Cats Cats Cats Cats

by JOHN R. GILBERT

PAUL HAMLYN
LONDON · NEW YORK · SYDNEY · TORONTO

CONTENTS

Page

PAUL HAMLYN

Published by
THE HAMLYN PUBLISHING
GROUP LTD.
Hamlyn House, The Centre,
Feltham, Middlesex
© Copyright 1961 Paul Hamlyn Ltd

First published 1961
Revised Edition 1969
Printed in Czechoslovakia
by Svoboda, Prague

About this Book

It goes without saying that a new book on cats will appeal, first and foremost, to the host of cat-lovers everywhere. This book makes no startling new revelations, nor advances any revolutionary theories. Neither is it a text-book, full of technical information about breeding, exhibition and general care of cats, although it touches upon all these subjects.

It is a book which sets out primarily to entertain, by word and picture — to portray the cat not only in his everyday moods and activities, but also in less familiar guises and surroundings. The approach is serious, but not solemn; the manner light-hearted, but not facetious. It attempts to set the cat in his proper perspective, against the backcloth of past events and in the changing pattern of life today.

The rewards of preaching to the converted, though gratifying, are modest. Perhaps, therefore, this book will find its way into the neutral camp, comprising those who protest that they have no strong feelings towards cats, either one way or the other; who endure cats, but neither condemn nor praise. It would be pleasant to think that the informal and non-specialised nature of this book could result in one or two positive converts.

As for the anti-cat brigade, it would be too much to hope that a few enchanting photographs or a handful of enlightening facts could radically alter their thoughts and feelings on the subject. But perhaps even they may be induced to think again, to give the cat a fair hearing, and to admit—if only to themselves—that the cat may, after all, have some virtues. It is a claim made in a spirit of humility rather than boastfulness.

The cat has had a violent and eventful history. It has been worshipped and it has been persecuted. Today it enjoys, and doubtless prefers, a position half-way between excessive adulation and senseless brutality. Obvious cruelty must, of course, be fought with all the weapons which a civilised community can muster. That battle is slowly being won. But cosseting and over-indulgence are also forms of cruelty, for the cat is a robust and hardy animal, not a mere article of adornment.

The cat's praises deserve to be sung, at times loudly. But it is not betraying the cause to admit occasionally to his shortcomings. We ought to incline towards moderation rather than exaggeration, both in our treatment and presentation of the cat, modelling ourselves on him; for he finds it more effective to insinuate rather than to bludgeon his way into our homes and hearts. For the rest, let the depth and variety of the cat's engaging personality be justification enough for this new book.

The Gayer-Anderson cat in the British Museum.

The Past of Cats

The cat's role in history

The domestic cat, as we know it today, stepped on to the stage of history at a relatively advanced date, but once having made an appearance it occupied a central position in more than one scene. Cats cannot exactly claim to have influenced the course of events or shaped the destiny of nations, but they have significantly 'hit the headlines' more often than any other domestic animal. More than once a nation has practically formulated an official policy towards them, and right through history there has been strong feeling for or against them, but seldom mere indifference. No doubt cats would have preferred to live quietly and unobtrusively, but circumstances seemed to conspire to bring them into the limelight, sometimes to their advantage, but more often to their detriment.

The heyday of the cat

Written and pictorial records show that the cat was a domestic pet in Egypt over four thousand years ago. It is possible that it was also a household favourite in India at about the same period, though there are only occasional references to cats in Sanscrit writings. With Egypt we are on more secure ground, and it is clear that the honoured position which cats occupied in society under the Pharaohs has never since been equalled.

The tomb paintings, frescoes and bronzes of Egyptian cats depict short-haired, tabby-like animals, sleek and long-legged, in shape not unlike the modern Abyssinian cats. Many experts feel certain that the Abyssinian cat of today is in fact descended from the celebrated Egyptian cat of home and temple, but this is only one of the many fascinating theories concerning the ancestry of modern breeds.

Whatever may have been its relationship to our own cats, or its own descent from wilder ancestors, it is evident that the cat was a devoted pet which was among the first possessions to be rescued in the event of a fire, and which threw the entire household into mourning when it died. More importantly, however, it was also one of the Egyptian sacred animals, a part of the whole divine order. The cat was sacred to the goddess Pasht or Bastet—some think the name 'puss' is derived from her—and along with jackals, baboons, crocodiles and other animals associated with deities, they were worshipped in her temples, paraded and garlanded on her feast days, and buried with much pomp and elaboration in her holy ground. The corpses of cats were frequently embalmed and mummified, and less than a century ago the remains of more than 300,000 mummified cats were discovered on the site of the Temple of Beni Hassan, built in honour of Bastet.

The Egyptians were quick to realise the immense value of cats in killing vermin. Farmers and merchants in particular found them staunch allies. So both from the practical and the religious points of view cats were accorded great respect and legal protection. The penalty for killing one of these sacred animals was death.

There is a famous story—nobody knows whether it actually happened—of the Roman soldier who was practically lynched by an enraged mob for having killed a cat accidentally. According to the historian Herodotus the incident was taken up in high diplomatic circles and was said to have been one of several provocative actions which sparked off the wars between Egypt and Rome.

An earlier invader of Egypt, Cambyses, son of Cyrus the Great of Persia, apparently turned the Egyptian devotion to cats to his own advantage when besieging the port of Pelusium. The legend is that he ordered some of his troops to carry live cats which he threatened to toss over the walls of the city if the Egyptians refused to surrender. The threat worked, and the defenders capitulated rather than condone such cruelty to their beloved animals.

Egyptian mummified cats in the British Museum.

7

Venturing farther afield

Although the Egyptians strictly forbade the export of their precious cats, they gradually made their way, by various methods and devious routes, eastward to the Orient and northward and westward into Europe. Egyptian monks, Phoenician and Greek traders all engaged in a lucrative smuggling business, and although the Egyptians sent out counter-agents in an effort to check the trade, they rapidly lost their prized monopoly. The cat was already known in China in 1000 B.C. and travelled on to Japan. Curiously, in both countries it was called 'Mau' or 'Mao', the name which the Egyptians gave to it.

By the fifth century the cat was popular in Persia, and wherever it was introduced in the Hindu, Mohammedan or Buddhist countries, there it was honoured and esteemed. In Burma and Siam, though many centuries later, the cat once again frequented palaces and temples, but without re-capturing its semi-devine status in the public mind. In Japan, so precious were cats that they were kept on leads until the year 1602. Then the government ordered them set loose, in which condition they were far more effective in combating the vermin which menaced the silk-worm industry.

By the beginning of the common era the cat was well established in Greece and Rome, although the Greeks do not appear to have set any special store by it. Doubtless they were more efficient mouse-catchers than the weasels which had been used until then, but they did not catch on as household pets, and only on one Greek vase is there a portrait of a cat. It is being led by a slave.

The Romans, however, adopted the cat as a symbol of liberty, and in the wake of Rome's invading armies the cat found its way into every corner of Europe. In Holland, for example, the old Roman stronghold of Cat Vicense is known nowadays as Kattewyk, or Cat's Town.

Britain probably owed its earliest knowledge of

Roman mosaic found at Pompeii, depicting a cat with a bird. (National Museum, Naples)

A Buddhist Priest in Japan with the Temple's pet cat. The strings of paper birds represent wishes for departed cats made by their late owners.

A Japanese cat-lover rubs the Wishing Stone to make sure her pets have gone to heaven, while the Temple Cat looks on.

the domestic cat to the Phoenicians who sailed to Cornwall to trade for tin, but later the Romans brought them in as well, as is proved by the discovery of the remains of a cat in a villa at Lullingstone, Kent. The Scots, too, kept cats, and there they became symbols of courage. County Caithness is the County of Cats. Appropriately enough, the Egyptian-type cat was conveyed to Scotland by King Fergus I, who traced his descent from the Greek commander of the Egyptian army which was swallowed up in the Red Sea at the time of Moses.

Wherever cats appeared they quickly established themselves as loyal friends and helpers, so much so that laws began to be enacted to protect them. The most famous piece of legislation was that introduced by the King of South Wales, Hywel Dda, in 936. This fixed the penalty for killing a cat at the equivalent of the cat's worth, meticulously measured in corn. On the Continent, too, cats figured among the most treasured possessions of princes and nobles.

The Crusaders brought back with them from the East beautiful long-haired cats which mingled with short-haired stock. They also brought back plague and pestilence. Now the cat's value was greatly enhanced, although it was not properly appreciated that rats and mice were the carriers. Even had there been a thousand times as many cats it is doubtful whether they could have done anything to check the spreading of the Black Death, which took such a frightful toll of human life in all the civilised lands of Europe.

Days of wrath

The cat's day of glory was, however, short-lived. During the Middle Ages its fortunes underwent a sudden and terrible reverse. A cult had grown up in the Rhineland in which cats played a prominent part; orgies were held, associated with the Norse goddess Freya, whose chariot was traditionally drawn by two black cats. These rites were regarded as undermining the foundations of the Church, and it was the Church which initiated the frightful counter-attacks which culminated in witch-hunts, torture and burning throughout Western and Northern Europe.

The persecution of witches was legalised by Pope Innocent VIII and the Inquisition. Merely to own

The returning Crusaders introduced the long-haired cat to the western world.

An Abyssinian, who many believe may be descended from the Egyptian sacred cats, suitably ornamented, as of old.

10

A Japanese print of a cat catching a mouse. (British Museum)

a cat was to risk arrest for sorcery. Superstition and mass hysteria knew no bounds. The cat was now linked with the Devil and unimaginable acts of darkness. Hundreds of thousands of innocent people were subjected to ghastly tortures and martyrdom on fabricated evidence or on mere hearsay, and where cats were found they were tortured and burned as well.

What made it all the more terrible was that this orgy of killing was carried out in the solemn name of religion. On Saint Days, such as the Festival of Saint John in France, sack-loads of cats were ritually burned in the bonfires. The Dauphin, Louis XIII, managed to stop the hideous proceedings temporarily, but the burnings were resumed by his son, Louis XIV. In Denmark and Belgium, even more fiendish torments were devised. Westwards the witch-hunting mania spread to England, and across the Atlantic to the colony of New England. The human toll was incalculable, and by decimating the cat population everywhere, authorities in their folly merely encouraged disease and plague to run riot.

Calm after storm

Eventually the panic subsided, and a semblance of sanity returned. In the newly-formed American colonies, the settlers found once more that cats were indispensable companions. Later, during the California Gold Rush, cats were imported from Europe at fantastic prices. The first cat to be imported into Paraguay in 1750 cost a pound of gold. Everywhere the tide began to turn again. Although many could not then, and cannot even today, rid themselves of prejudice based on ancient superstition, cats were gradually restored to the favour of intelligent people in all parts of the world.

In France especially, as if to make amends for centuries of cruelty, cats became the favourites of cardinals, statesmen, scientists and men of letters. Today, famous men and women in all walks of life make no secret of the sense of companionship which they derive from their cats; and in warehouses, dockyards, ministries, museums, theatres, schools, post-offices, ships and farmyards, cats are getting their own back—enjoying once again, if with less pomp and ceremony, something of that popular esteem which their ancestors accepted as their unquestioned due in Egypt four thousand years ago.

The Laws of Howel the Good, Prince of South Wales

The worth of a cat and her tiethi (qualities) is this:

1. The worth of a kitten from the night it is kittened until it shall open its eyes is a legal penny.

2. And from that time, until it shall kill mice, two legal pence.

3. And after it shall kill mice, four legal pence; and so it always remains.

4. Her tiethi are, to see, to hear, to kill mice, to have her claws entire, to rear and not devour her kittens, and if she be bought, and be deficient in any one of these tiethi; let one third of her worth be returned.

Of Cats:

1. The worth of a cat that is killed or stolen: its head to be put downwards upon a clean even floor, with its tail lifted upwards, and thus suspended, whilst wheat is poured about it, until the tip of its tail be covered; and that is to be its worth; if the corn cannot be had a milch sheep, with her lamb and her wool, is its value; if it be a cat which guards the King's barn.

2. The worth of a common cat is four legal pence.

3. Whoever shall sell a cat is to answer for her not going a caterwauling every moon; and that she devour not her kittens; and that she have ears, eyes, teeth and nails; and being a good mouser.

Tabbies

A selection of short- and long-haired tabbies in pensive moods.

Although there are Brown Tabbies, Red Tabbies and Silver Tabbies, the Browns are by far the commonest, and you will rarely see a stray Silver in the streets. But let nobody dismiss the tabbies as ordinary 'alley-cats' for they have won their fair share of awards at championship shows everywhere.

The word 'tabby' seems to be derived from a district in old Baghdad called Attabiah, where a special kind of silk was manufactured, with a distinctive watered effect, not unlike the subtle markings of modern tabbies.

The tabbies have a strong claim to be considered among the world's oldest breeds, as is clearly shown by early Egyptian paintings. Even some of the modern luxury breeds probably have tabby blood in them, for their kittens frequently show indisputable tabby markings at birth.

More tabbies – en famille, and in serious and light-hearted vein.

A child's-eye view of a black cat.

This baby's favourite plaything is the family cat.

Children and Cats

A group of Japanese children allow the cat to take pride of place.

This beautiful cream Persian is nearly as big as his proud mistress.

Six baby Siamese romping with one baby girl, and enjoying it too.

The Order

of

the Bath

Why don't you join me in the bath? The water's delicious.

No sooner do I get you dry than you start cleaning yourself all over again.

Changed your mind, eh?

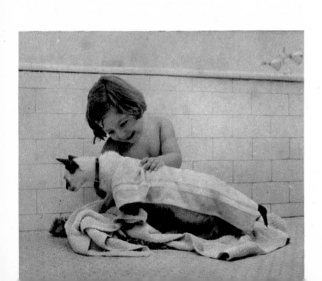

From the Cat's Viewpoint

This is my Man. I'm not afraid of him.

He is very powerful, for he eats a lot; he is All-eating. What are you eating? Give me some!

He is not beautiful, because he has no fur. Not having sufficient saliva he has to wash himself with water. He miaows with a gruff voice, and much too often. Sometimes he purrs in his sleep.

Open the door for me.

I don't know why he became the Master; he must have eaten something magnificent.

He doesn't mess up my rooms.

He takes into his paw a black sharp claw and uses it to engrave white leaves. He can't play in any other way. He sleeps at night instead of in the day, he can't see in the dark, he has no delights. He never thinks of blood, never dreams of the hunt and of the fray, never does he sing with love.

Often during the night when I hear magic and mysterious voices, when I see how everything is becoming alive with the darkness, HE sits at the table with bowed head and all the time, he scratches with that black claw at the white leaves. You mustn't believe that I care about you. I only hear the soft rustling of your claw. Sometimes the rustling stops, the poor dull head doesn't know now any more how to play, and then I feel sorry for him, and I deign to approach and miaow softly in sweet and tantalizing discord. Then my Man lifts me up and buries his warm face in my fur. Just then, for a second a flash of higher existence awakens in him, and he sighs with bliss and purrs something which is almost understandable.

But you mustn't believe that I care about you. You have warmed me, and now again I shall go and listen to the dark voices.

Karel Čapek. *I Had a Dog and a Cat*
(Translated M. and R. Weatherall)

Calling all Persians

My goodness, you're tall

The Cat and the Moon

The cat went here and there
And the moon spun round like a top,
And the nearest kin of the moon,
The creeping cat, looked up.
Black Minnaloushe stared at the moon,
For, wander and wail as he would,
The pure cold light in the sky
Troubled his animal blood.
Minnaloushe runs in the grass
Lifting his delicate feet.
Do you dance, Minnaloushe, do you dance?
When two close kindred meet,
What better than call a dance?
Maybe the moon may learn,
Tired of that courtly fashion,
A new dance turn.
Minnaloushe creeps through the grass
From moonlit place to place,
The sacred moon overhead
Has taken a new phase.
Does Minnaloushe know that his pupils
Will pass from change to change,
And that from round to crescent
From crescent to round they range?
Minnaloushe creeps through the grass
Alone, important and wise,
And lifts to the changing moon
His changing eyes.

(William Butler Yeats)

Curve of elegance

British Blue.

The Pattern of Cats

Aristocrats and nondescripts

There is one advantage in trying to decide what kind of cat you want to keep, namely that the choice is not tremendously wide. There are so many considerations in buying a dog—this one will be too large for a flat in town, that one will be unpredictable with the children, another will be delicate, nervous and prone to ailments. You may yearn secretly for a Labrador or an Alsatian, but you will probably have to settle for a Pekinese or a Dachshund.

Cats also have their varying moods and temperaments, but selecting one is child's play by comparison. For one thing, they are all more or less the same size. A large cat is not five times as large as a small one. Some of them have short tails, some have long, some have round heads, others have wedge-shaped. Some are prettier, more affectionate, even more intelligent than others. But most of them are reasonably undemanding and untemperamental, fairly adaptable with regard to surroundings, children and other animals—and quite useless for any other purpose than to catch the occasional mouse and provide companionship.

The Governing Council of the Cat Fancy in Great Britain lists over thirty recognised breeds, which should provide a fairly broad scope for any prospective buyer, but the truth is that unless you are interested in breeding and exhibiting cats you will never set eyes on half this number outside the show cages. Blue Creams and Silver Tabbies are too precious to be allowed to roam the back gardens and farmyards.

Out of an estimated cat population in Britain of around twelve million—and in the United States the figure is nearer twenty-one million—the vast majority are short-haired cats. They may be black, white, grey, ginger, tabby, black and white, tabby and white, tortoiseshell, and other colour combinations. All they have in common is that it would be impossible to trace back their ancestry very far. They do not possess an impressive pedigree, they would not win any prizes at a show because they have the wrong markings or the wrong-coloured eyes, they come and go as they please and do not have to worry too much about their appearance. Where sheer numbers are concerned, they are more truly representative of the cat populace than the aristocrats of the show bench, and when we talk about the different breeds of cats we should never forget the ordinary 'household' cats, who refuse to fit into any rigid category.

The long and short of it

Domestic cats are conveniently divided into long-haired and short-haired varieties. This is accepted

Long-haired Silver Tabby.

Seal-pointed Siamese.

Short-haired White.

all over the world. In Britain there is a further sub-division of the short-haired breeds, into British and Foreign. The latter is somewhat misleading, since although most of the breeds within this category may originally have come from abroad, the finest specimens nowadays are bred in Britain and many are exported. The difference is chiefly one of body structure and coat pattern.

The long-haired cats are considered by many—including some owners of short-haired varieties—to be over-indulged, indolent creatures. The picture is a false one. Any cat may be over-indulged, and as a result become fat and lazy. Most people who take the trouble to own long-haired cats, and who are prepared to devote that little extra care and attention which their silky fur demands, are fully aware of the dangers of pampering them, and know them to be far from lazy or unresponsive. The length of their fur prevents them from moving about as rapidly as their short-haired cousins, but their reactions are every bit as quick, their intelligence is equally keen and their natures just as affectionate. Furthermore, their elegance and beauty cannot be denied.

The long-haired breeds are now commonly known as Persians, though previously called Angoras. They were first imported into England from Italy in the sixteenth century and have no connection nowadays with Central Asia. They have a stocky, low-lying body with short thickish legs, a broad rounded head with small tufted ears set well apart, a tiny flattened nose and round intent eyes. The entire body is covered with a long silky coat, and a handsome frill or ruff surrounds the head. The tail is short and full.

The so-called British short-haired breeds have a slim, vigorous body of medium length, neat and well-proportioned legs with round feet, a round head with smallish ears, a short nose, large round eyes and a short thick tail. The Foreign types have an even longer body, very lithe and flexible, with rather longer legs, small feet and a long tapering tail. The head is wedge-shaped, the tall ears ideally forming a straight line with the muzzle, and the eyes are slanting and oriental.

The Persians may have had a common wild ancestor in Central Asia, or they may simply be variations of short-haired types. Nobody really knows. The texture of a cat's fur may come about as suddenly and as accidentally as a new coat colour. In recent years, for example, a number of Rex or curly-coated cats have been successfully bred, and it may well be that in a decade or so curly-coated cats will be a common sight, in a variety of colours.

Chinchilla kittens.

Abyssinian.

Russian Blue.

Birmans.

Coats of many colours

The earliest domestic cats, as far as we can judge from paintings, were tabbies, and although opinions differ as to the origin of the word, the term is loosely used nowadays for any complex pattern of stripes and blotches. The true tabby marking, however, is very distinctive. It applies both to the long and short-haired varieties and the pattern extends down the length of the back and sides of the body, joining underneath. The rings on the tail are even and regular, the head and cheeks are lightly marked, with an 'M' on the forehead, and there is a butterfly-shaped mark on the shoulder. Small wonder that the ideal show tabby should be difficult to breed, whether in Brown, Red or Silver.

The 'self' or single-colour cats include Whites, Blacks, Creams, Blues, Reds, Smokes and Chinchillas.

The true Reds are much richer than ginger, and the genuine Blues are blue and not merely off-grey. The Whites, Blacks, Creams and Blues are recognised both as long and short-haired breeds, the others only as long-haired. This is a bit confusing, and only of significance for show purposes. There are of course myriads of short-haired black cats prowling about, but most of them have green eyes and flecks of white here and there; show standards call for orange eyes and jet black fur all over. The long-haired Smoke must have a black coat shading to silver on the sides, short-haired whites must have blue eyes, long-haired whites either blue or orange,

Blue-pointed Siamese.

A mixed litter – two Black and a Smoke.

and so on. Curiously, most blue-eyed whites are deaf from birth, although their perceptions and movements are astonishingly alert.

Among the Persians the most popular varieties and the most common are the Blues and the Chinchillas. The former has been exhibited in Britain for seventy years and is an equal favourite overseas; the copper or orange eyes are most striking against the evenly blue coat. Many people consider the Chinchilla to be even more handsome, with its black-tipped white undercoat and blue-green eyes. A similar variety, the Shaded Silver, is also extremely popular in America and parts of the Commonwealth.

The cats with coats of two colours or more are even rarer. Although the description 'tortoiseshell' is freely bandied about, it is very seldom that one sees a perfect specimen, either in the long or short-haired classes. The true Tortoiseshell is black, red and cream in fairly equal proportions, whilst the Tortoiseshell-and-white has white in addition to these three shades. The patches of colour should, in the best specimens, be unblurred. There is more trial and error involved with these breeds than with any others, and for some reason most Tortoiseshells and Tortoiseshell-and-whites are females. So, too, are the long-haired Blue-creams, which are often the result of mating Blue with Cream, or Blue with Tortoiseshell.

The Manx cats are in a class of their own, although superficially akin to the British short-hairs. They come in a variety of colours, including white, but most of them are tabbies. Where a tail would normally appear, there is only a hollow. The high back legs of the Manx give it a rabbit-like appearance, and it moves with rabbit-like hops, but there the resemblance ends. Despite the absence of tail, the Manx cat is a confident climber, an expert rodent-hunter and fisherman, a courageous and affectionate pet.

Brown Tabby.

Short-haired Black.

A Chartreux or Carthusian cat.

'Foreign' favourites

There is always heated argument when it comes to deciding which varieties are the true aristocrats of the cat world. Some say the Blue Persians and the Chinchillas, others plump for the Foreign short-haired breeds. To the ordinary cat-lover, it hardly seems worth coming to blows about it, however healthy competition is supposed to be. Still, it is undeniable that Siamese cats are gaining in popularity every year, and that more and more people are succumbing to the attractions of the Burmese and Abyssinians, though these two breeds are still limited in numbers. All of these have in common a sleek and graceful silhouette, keen intelligence and an exceptionally affectionate nature.

Siamese cats were first introduced into Britain in 1884, and until then had been closely guarded—especially the males—by the Siamese authorities. Today they are bred in many countries and several handsome new varieties have appeared. Ideally, they should possess uniformly-coloured coats, either pale fawn or brown. In the best-known type, the Seal-pointed, the 'points', that is the muzzle, ears, feet and tail, are dark brown; the Chocolate-pointed Siamese have chocolate-coloured points, the Blue-pointed dark blue, the Lilac-pointed pinkish-grey. Of these, only the Lilac-pointed is not so far a recognised breed in Britain, but this is doubtless only a question of time, for it already forms a separate breed in America. Red-pointed Siamese cats are also being successfully reared, and there is no reason why there should be any limit to the number of colours still capable of being developed. There is already much talk of Tortoise-shell-points and Gold-points, and the prospects are most intriguing.

All Siamese cats have the distinctive wedge-shaped heads and slanting eyes, some have squints and others kinks in their tails. They crave human company more than most other cats, are exceptionally devoted pets and are remarkably talkative. Their peculiar squawks and child-like whimperings are not always appreciated by neighbours.

Burmese cats are fast winning acclaim, and deservedly. Although fairly common in North America for thirty years, the first pair to be seen in Britain arrived from the United States in 1947, and the breed was only officially recognised in 1952. The Burmese cat is obviously closely linked with the Siamese, but whether it is a variation of the Siamese or vice-versa is disputable. There does not seem to be any proof that it even originated in Burma, though the first female imported into America came from Rangoon. The coat of the

Shaded Silver Persian.

Manx.

Black Persian.

Burmese cat is rich deep brown, with a high polish, its eyes may be either green or yellow, and it is known for its placid and affectionate nature.

The Abyssinian cats are also prized by connoisseurs, but are still comparatively rare owing to their not being prolific breeders. They came to Britain from Africa in 1868, and were recognised as a separate breed as early as 1882. As might be expected, they were never at any time imported from Abyssinia. Some authorities hail the Abyssinian as the genuine descendant of the Egyptian sacred cat, others maintain that it is the result of random tabby matings. But sacred or not, it is a stately creature, with its long body, and soft

Long-haired Tortoiseshell-and-White.

Blue Persian.

ruddy-brown coat with bands of 'ticked' hairs—hairs with dark brown or black tips. The show standards state that no white should appear anywhere, but most specimens have white lips and chins. Abyssinian cats have gentle, subdued voices and loving dispositions.

The Russian Blues, once called Archangel Blues or Foreign Blues, may once have been pets of the Imperial Tsars, though the less romantically inclined deny that they have any Russian blood in their veins. They were recognised in Britain as a separate breed in 1948. They are lovely animals, with a unique, seal-like, close-fitting coat, varying in colour from medium to dark blue.

Orange-eyed White Persian.

A litter of Cream and Blue Cream Persian kittens.

33

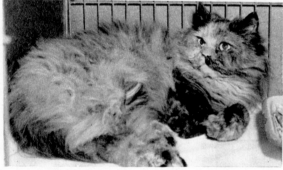

Burmese.

Havana – Chestnut Brown Foreign.

Long-haired Tortoiseshell.

Newcomers

Patient experiment has recently introduced two new and striking breeds, the Havana or Chestnut Brown Foreign, and the long-haired Colourpoint. The former, owing no allegiance to Cuba, is a purely British breed, having a mahogany or chestnut-coloured coat and slanting green eyes. The latter is already very popular in the United States and Canada, where it is known as Himalayan. It has a flowing, cream-coloured coat with dark brown points and rounded blue eyes. This beautiful cat therefore has the coat texture of a Persian and the colour features of a Siamese. It is not, nevertheless, a long-haired Siamese, despite the fact that attempts have been made to produce such a cat.

One other unusual cat which has not been shown in Britain is the Burmese 'Sacred' cat, or Burman, not to be confused with the short-haired Burmese. It is a long-haired cat, of legendary but probably imaginary sacred descent, very popular in France. It has a long body, with Siamese-type colouring, coat slightly golden, dark points and white-tipped paws; again a blend of Siamese and Persian, but not sacrificing the individual qualities of either.

In America and the Commonwealth several other breeds are known and exhibited, such as the Shaded Silver Persian and, in the States, the Peke-faced cat. Here the face resembles that of a Pekinese dog, but in other ways the animal conforms to normal long-hair standards. They are a popular breed and are exhibited under Red and Red Tabby classes.

The picture is changing all the time. Selective breeding and haphazard mating will result in new coat textures, new colour combinations, maybe even new shapes. The more variety the better. Not everybody wants or can afford a Russian Blue or a Silver Tabby. To most people, the ordinary household cat, however mongrel, is companion enough. So let the controversy rage about their comparative virtues—they care least of all. They are just cats, and there is a bond, mysterious and intangible, impossible to define in terms of mere shape and colour, which links them all.

Rex, or Curly-coated.

Long-haired Red Tabby.

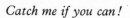

Catch me if you can!

Sorry, this pocket's occupied.

Enough To Make a Cat Laugh

A beauty-queen from the Danish island of Bornholm.

I've cut down to five a day.

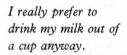

Jump to it!

Then that's one medium and one under-done.

I really prefer to drink my milk out of a cup anyway.

Watch out for that knight!

A Cat May Look on a King

The proverbs relating to cats are legion, and the curious thing about them is the way they turn up, in only slightly varying forms, in countries as far apart as Albania and China. This makes it next to impossible to trace the true origin of any single proverb. Some of them date back over a thousand years, others appear to have been coined during the present century. The following is only a small selection of proverbs and quotations, many of them existing in more than half a dozen different forms.

- The cat is hungry when a crust of bread contents her.
- He that denies the cat skimmed milk must give the mouse cream.
- A lame cat is better than a swift horse when rats infest the palace.
- A gloved cat was never a good hunter.
- The cat does not catch mice for God.
- There are more ways of killing a cat than choking her with cream.
- An old cat knows fresh milk.
- The more you stroke a cat, the more it lifts its tail.
- The cat makes sure whose chin it may lick.
- Thou can'st have no more of the cat but his skinne.
- To please himself only a cat purrs.
- It has been the providence of nature to give this creature nine lives instead of one.
- Never was cat or dog drowned that could but see the shore.
- A cat pent up becomes a lion.
- A cat is a lion in a jungle of small bushes.
- Weill wats the mouse, the cat's oot of the house.
- When all candles be out, all cats be grey.
- Who dare bell the cat?
- The cat loves fish but does not wish to wet its feet.
- Never put the kit to watch your chickens.

Determination

Face of innocence

Feline inscrutability

The Power of Cats

A bronze figure of Bastet holding a sistrum.
(British Museum)

Good or bad luck?

'See which way the cat jumps', 'Let the cat out of the bag', 'Raining cats and dogs', 'No room to swing a cat'—how frequently and glibly we use such phrases and dozens of others. We sprinkle our conversation with them in the most natural and unthinking manner. Probably the cat has inspired ten times as many of these popular tags as has any other animal.

Yet they are not empty or meaningless. If we stop to examine them more closely we find that many of them have their roots and explanations in history or folk-lore, dating back in particular to the days when the cat was held sacred, or later still, to the time when it was tortured as an ally of the devil.

Throughout the centuries the cat has been an emblem both of good and of bad luck. In some countries it has been a personification of the devil himself, in others a charm to ward off those same evil spirits. It controls and prophesies the weather, it is consulted before setting off on an expedition, it cures afflictions and diseases.

The cat has been revered and spurned, fêted and reviled. Even today a black cat symbolises good fortune for one person, bad for another. It is useless to search for some consistency in these everyday sayings. You might just as well try to discover some overwhelming generalisation which will embrace all aspects of the cat's deep, perplexing personality.

A creature divine

Cats were tamed only a few thousand years ago and we know well what a supreme place of honour they occupied in Egypt under the Pharaohs. Bastet, the goddess who assumed their likeness and with whom they were most closely identified, represented pleasure, fertility and maternity. From birth to death cats were treated as semi-divine creatures with undoubted other-worldly powers.

Cats, however, were also associated with some of the higher Egyptian deities, such as Isis, who symbolised life itself, and Osiris, who set the sun on its daily course. The historian Plutarch stated that for the Egyptians a male cat represented the sun and a female the moon. There is a famous tomb painting which shows the Great Cat Ra devouring the snake-dragon of darkness. During eclipses, those periods of conflict between the forces of light and darkness, people used to shake their sistrums, musical instruments upon which were perched figures of female cats. This tumult was designed to spur on the cat-goddess in her struggle with the evil forces of night.

It is thought that the cat may have been a domestic pet in India at about the same early age and certainly cats were common in China about 3000 years ago. It is not, therefore, surprising that in Asiatic countries cats have always enjoyed popularity and esteem. Mohammedans, Hindus

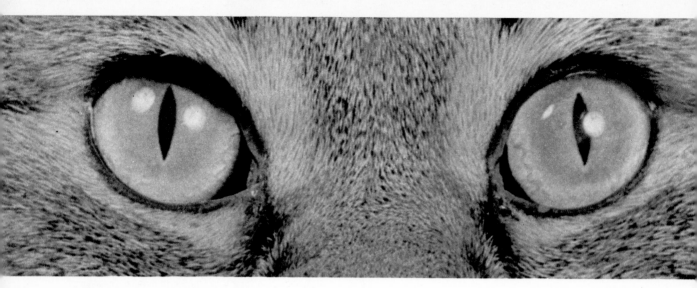

The hypnotic gaze of a cat.

and Buddhists all treat cats with love and consideration, and wherever cats appear in Eastern myths and folk-lore it is practically always in a pleasant context. Only the Japanese appear to possess devil cats and even they do not seem to be terribly sinister animals.

The Mohammedans are responsible for the quaint legend about the origin of the common cat, which made its appearance in Noah's ark when the lion sneezed. Chinese legend has it that the cat was a cross between a lioness and a monkey. In Siam a blue-eyed cat was supposed to represent silver, a yellow-eyed cat gold. Whether cats were ever really temple animals in Siam or Burma is open to question, but because of the Buddhist belief in the sanctity of all forms of animal life, cats have been traditionally accepted and appreciated in the East in a manner entirely unknown in the West.

Necklaces from ancient Egypt, with animal charms. The lowest one represents the hippopotamus, the two others cats.
(British Museum)

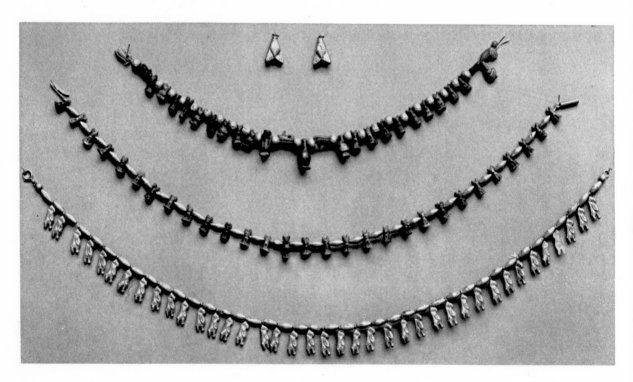

No wonder some people are scared of cats!

Sun, moon and storm

In the Western hemisphere the cat rapidly lost its divine status. Although Tiberius Gracchus set its image on the Temple of Liberty in Rome, neither Greeks nor Romans credited it with supernatural powers. Yet somehow the cat could never be considered on quite the same level as man's faithful friend, the dog, or his docile servant, the horse. People persisted in seeing in the cat some vestiges of supernatural influence, and it soon assured itself of a prominent position in the folk-lore of many lands.

The Egyptians and Chinese, for example, were the first to introduce the theory that the cat's eyes

A Roman floor mosaic discovered at Orange, France, depicting a black cat. (Victoria and Albert Museum)

45

The witch-doctor of the tribe.

A Japanese print showing a cat beneath a full moon. (British Museum)

Part of an Early Ming Chinese painting by Chao Yuan of a tiger and her cubs. (British Museum)

waxed and waned according to the phases of the moon. The Chinese held that by examining the eyes of a cat you could accurately tell the time. Moreover, the influence of the cycles of the sun and the moon, and of the ebb and flow of the tides upon the cat's eyes was not a theory confined to one place or one period. Nor did the passage of time and scientific enlightenment correct this curious notion. In 1607, the English writer Edmund Topsell, in his *Historie of Foure-Footed Beastes,* repeated it all at some length. 'The Egyptians,' he wrote, 'have observed in the eyes of the Cat, the encrease of the Moonlight for with the Moone, they shine more fully at the ful, and more dimly in the change and wain, and the male cat doth vary his eyes with the sunne; for when the sun ariseth, the apple of his eye is long; towards noon it is round, and at the evening it cannot be seene at all, but the whole eye showeth alike.'

These beliefs are not as ridiculous as they sound, for the pupils of cats' eyes do enlarge and contract according to the intensity of light, though there is nothing supernatural about that. Yet many people still admit to finding the unwinking gaze of the cat 'uncanny', and there are others who persistently overrate their visual powers. It is difficult to convince such people, for instance, that, good as a cat's vision is, it cannot see in pitch darkness.

As for the cat's influence on the weather, that always was and still is widely believed. In certain parts of England, it is said that if a cat turns its tail towards the fire, frost is due, and if it licks its tail, rain is on the way. To seamen, black cats are notoriously unlucky, bringers of foul weather and disaster, whereas tortoiseshell cats are lucky, and in parts of the Far East are sent up the mastheads to put the storm devils to flight. In Lapland, the household cat is solemnly consulted about weather prospects before a long journey is undertaken.

Here again it is not hard to understand how some of these curious beliefs arose, for cats do behave in extraordinary ways in certain types of weather, being hyper-sensitive to changes of atmosphere. Before a storm they often display signs of acute nervousness and tension, settling down only when the thunder and lightning begin. To this extent they may perhaps be regarded as weather guides. Moreover, there are countless stories of cats whose extra-keen senses have enabled them to give warning of fires and other natural disasters and whose presence has led to the saving of human lives. Close observation of their behaviour at such times may well account for their being credited with supernatural powers of prediction and premonition which they do not really possess.

Detail of a Roman mosaic, depicting a horse and cat, from the Piazza Armerina, Sicily.

Sorcerer's apprentice

In the Middle Ages, the cat saw its blackest days. Countless numbers of innocent people went to the stake for no better reason than that they owned cats. Witches and their cats were held responsible for any local misfortune, whether it was a crop failure, a miscarriage, a sudden death or an epidemic. It was a logical conclusion that the cat must be allied with the devil, might even be the devil himself. So it seemed only prudent to stamp out the evil by any means available; and it was centuries before reason and humanity put a stop to the dreadful proceedings.

One medieval book entitled *Beware the Cat* solemnly warned that it was useless killing only one cat, since a witch was capable of taking on the guises of nine different cats in succession. This sort of rubbish was widely believed and acted upon. In many places full-dress trials of cats on charges of sorcery took place. A fair trial evidently was a sufficient salve for the conscience.

It would be pleasant to record that once this frenzy was over the cat was speedily restored to its ancient pedestal of love and respect. Unfortunately, isolated instances of senseless brutality continued. J.G. Frazer, in his monumental book on myth and folklore, *The Golden Bough*, lists several occasions in France and Germany where cats, representing the corn-spirits, were ritually garlanded and then sacrificed at harvest time. Nor is it so long since cats were shut into hot stoves to ensure good fortune, or walled up in new buildings to protect the dwelling from natural catastrophes. Superstition, even in allegedly civilised communities, is a long time dying.

In a small village in the English Cotswolds there is a fascinating museum depicting witch craft through the ages. There is one model showing the kitchen of a Lancashire witch, complete with black cat. She is said to have died as recently as 1928. So who is to say whether even witchcraft is dead?

Despite all this, however, it would be foolish to lose our sense of proportion entirely. The tide has genuinely turned in the cat's favour, and its popularity is increasing steadily. We realise that the cat needs, above all else, affection and understanding. If some of us like to indulge in fanciful notions about its magical powers, no great harm will result—so long, that is, as we keep in mind the grim lesson of history.

In all probability, the cat will always stand in the popular mind as an ambiguous figure of good and bad luck, fair and foul weather, prosperity and penury. Not even the ancient Egyptians were entirely consistent about their cats. There is no good reason why we should be either.

47

The Old Woman and her Cats

A wrinkled hag, of wicked fame

Beside a little smoky flame

Sat hov'ring, pinched with age and frost;

Her shrivell'd hands, with veins embossed,

. . . .

About her swarm'd a num'rous brood

Of Cats, who lank with hunger mew'd.

Teaz'd with their cries her choler grew,

And thus she sputter'd. Hence, ye crew.

Fool that I was to entertain

Such imps, such fiends, a hellish train!

Had ye been never hous'd and nurs'd

I, for a witch, had ne'er been curs'd.

To you I owe, that crowds of boys

Worry me with eternal noise;

Straws laid across my pace retard,

The horse-shoe's nail'd (each threshold's guard).

The stunted broom the wenches hide,

For fear that I should up and ride.

. . . .

Replies a Cat. Let's come to proof.

Had we ne'er starved beneath your roof

We had, like others of our race,

In credit liv'd, as beasts of chase.

'Tis infamy to serve a hag;

Cats are thought imps, her broom a nag;

And boys against our lives combine,

Because, 'tis said, your cats have nine.

(John Gay. *Fables*)

Siamese

Siamese cats seem determined to be different. Their voices are unique, harsh, far-carrying and used with great variety and frequency. Many of them have thieving habits, all of them are immensely attached to their owners, easily and quickly upset by rebukes or by neglect. They are fastidiously clean, fight more fiercely than other breeds and seem to be proner to certain illnesses. But despite the amount of attention which they require both in sickness and in health, they are among the most entertaining and affectionate cats anywhere.

They are prolific breeders and five or six kittens usually appear in every litter. The colour of the coat tends to darken with age, and the distinctive mask does not appear completely until the kittens are almost grown up.

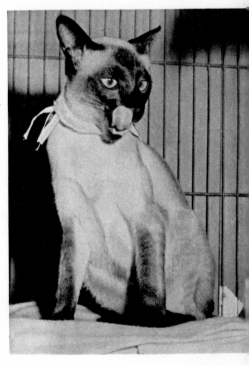

The Perfection of Cats

Organising the cats

Towards the end of the nineteenth century, the cat world began to get itself organised. The cat was once more an established household pet, and serious attention was being devoted to the breeding and public exhibition of pedigree cats. In 1871, the first official cat show took place at Crystal Palace in London, and in 1887 the National Cat Club was founded, with Harrison Weir as President. The Club kept a register of pedigree cats, fixed standards of points for all recognised breeds and issued a stud book in 1893.

As happens with most new organisations, criticism and opposition developed behind the scenes and within a few years a rival organisation, the Cat Club, was set up. This group lasted barely ten years. Out of the conflict, and benefiting from this early violent experience, arose the Cat Fanciers' Association in 1908, to which all groups, including the original National Cat Club, eventually became affiliated.

The Governing Council of the Cat Fancy emerged two years later. Today some twenty-three clubs in Britain are affiliated to it, not counting similar organisations abroad. The Governing Council is the feline equivalent of the Kennel Club, and has virtually complete control over pedigree breeding and exhibition. All affiliated clubs are entitled to send elected delegates to the Governing Council in proportion to their memberships.

The function of the Governing Council of the Cat Fancy is to encourage and promote interest in pedigree breeding. It keeps a national register of pedigree animals, issues an annual stud book, and supervises all commercial transactions, whether local or long-distance. Only cats and kittens registered with the Governing Council are eligible for exhibition at licensed shows, and it is the Governing Council which makes the rules for such shows and awards the championship certificates.

During the fifty years of its existence the Governing Council of the Cat Fancy has rightly set itself high standards and this has been one of the chief reasons why British bred cats are today in strong demand from all parts of the world. Many of the champions who have appeared at shows in the United States, Canada, South Africa, Australia and elsewhere have been descended from British stock.

Wherever cats have gained national popularity it has been found necessary to put matters on an official footing, and many clubs and societies have been formed, performing the same functions as those of the Governing Council in Britain. In places where the geographical areas are immense, it is obviously impossible for any single organisation to exercise sole control, and a number of local organisations share the work. In America, for example, the parent organisations, to which all local clubs are affiliated, are the American Cat Association, the Cat Fanciers' Association and the

'Buffins', winner of the title of 'Cat with the Most Appealing Expression' in 1958.

Cat Fanciers' Federation. Canadian Cat Clubs also come under the wing of one or other of these groups.

The first club in Australia was formed in 1925, and each state now has its separate organisations and shows. New Zealand's Governing Council was established in 1930, and the South African Cat Union in 1946.

It is interesting to note that the first independent cat show in the United States took place in 1895 and was organised by an Englishman. Since then there has been a continuous mutual exchange of livestock and information. America has imported prize-winning cats from Britain to improve its native stock, and Britain in turn is indebted to America for the introduction of the now-popular Burmese cat.

The various official organisations are responsible for bestowing formal recognition upon new breeds once they are considered to have gone past the experimental stage and to be sufficiently well established. This explains why a breed may have official status in one country and not in another.

The pick of the bunch

It is at the various Championship Shows that breeders, owners and the general public can keep abreast of the latest developments in the cat world. Here are gathered the most perfect specimens of each breed, competing against one another in their own classes, coveting the certificates which may one day entitle them to be called Champions.

The procedure varies from country to country. Where the climatic conditions permit, shows are held in the open and may last several days, with competitors travelling thousands of miles if need be. They are gay and colourful occasions, and the shows in Britain, invariably held indoors, are sedate by comparison. These are organised during the autumn and winter months, with the exception of the kitten shows which take place in the summer. The numerous shows organised by the different clubs, under the auspices of the Governing Council, attract huge entries, and the most expert and fully qualified judges conduct the proceedings with a scrupulous sense of fairness.

The rewards to be won at these shows are measured in terms of prestige rather than money. The prize money itself is negligible, a few pounds at most. What are keenly competed for are the Cups awarded by the various clubs for their own members in their separate classes, and the Certificates awarded to the best male and female of each breed in open

A litter of Russian Blue kittens at the annual show of the Kensington Kitten and Neuter Cat Club.

'Thiepvale Phoenix', a competitor at the Blue Persian Cat Society Show at Westminster in 1958.

Another prize-winner, 'Trelystan Olivine', in the Any Variety Long-haired or Short-haired Neuter class, at the National Cat Club Championship Show, in 1955.

An attractive litter of Siamese kittens at the 1959 National Cat Club Championship Show.

competition. To become a fully-fledged Champion, which entitles it to have the word 'Champion' prefixed to its name, a cat must win three separate Challenge Certificates under three different judges. After that the cat may compete in championship shows abroad, and to become an International Champion is to attain the highest pinnacle of exhibition fame.

A cat which does not belong to one of the recognised breeds may be entered under 'Any Other Colour' in the case of long-haired varieties, or 'Any Other Variety' in the case of short-haired cats. The latter class attracts many splendid entries and there is nothing to prevent a black-and-white or ginger-and-white cat from winning the highest awards. At some shows there are also opportunities for non-registered household pets and side classes for novices, juniors, etc.

Judy Grinham, the famous swimmer, holds 'Bonavia Anne', prize-winning Chinchilla at the National Cat Club's 1959 Show at Olympia.

The Rev. Basil Reese judging a British Blue cat at the Kensington Kitten and Neuter Cat Club's 1958 show.

53

The big day

Exhibiting a cat at one of these shows can be a nerve-wracking experience for owner and competitor alike. Some cats approach such ordeals as certain fortunate schoolchildren face critical examinations, accepting the unnatural routine with perfect calm and assurance, especially if they are old hands at the game. Others, less fortunate, have all the necessary qualifications, but are let down by their nerves on the vital day.

The regulations which are laid down by the Governing Council and which are provided, together with entry forms, by the individual show managers, are strict but sensible. Breach of the regulations may lead to disqualification. There are clear instructions governing each stage of the proceedings—travel, transport, grooming, feeding and display.

The shows themselves are conducted under the most rigid hygienic conditions. Each cat must be examined by a veterinary surgeon before being accepted for show. Every precaution is taken in the exhibition hall to avoid infection, and there is a compulsory three week interval between successive shows to make absolutely certain.

*A delightful litter
of mixed kittens.*

*A litter of very rare
two-months-old
Manx kittens.*

*'Purring Tom Kitten', winner of the Silver
Tabby or Smoke Class in the Seven
Counties Cat Club Championship Show in 1953.*

Compared with a dog show, the exhibition hall is a haven of peace, although there is a good deal of turmoil and tumult in the early stages. The competitors are placed in pens, twenty-four inches square, and there they remain the entire day, only being removed for a short period during the actual judging. No names are affixed to the pens, and the cats wear numbered tallies round their necks for identification. During the judging all owners are required to leave the hall.

After the early morning bustle the atmosphere becomes civilised and dignified, but tension runs high as the day wears on. Eventually the award cards are fixed to the pens of the prize-winners. There is jubilation for some, lamentation for others; and the judges are available when it is all over to discuss with successful and unsuccessful owners alike the reasons for their decisions.

All an exhibitor can do is to see that his or her cat is at the peak of condition for the show. Pre-show training may be valuable to accustom a cat to cramped conditions, but the physical condition of a cat is more important than its mental state. No cat in poor or middling shape can hope to win a prize.

Siamese cats await the judges.

'Mark of Allington' won two titles at the National Cat Club Show in 1953, 'Best Long-haired' and 'Best Cat in the Show'.

'Bayhorne Adam' was the Champion of Champions, and he guards his title fiercely.

'Woburn Monsieur', a Cream Persian, and winner of the title Best Long-haired Cat in the Show at the Croydon Cat Club Championship Show in 1957.

Points that matter

The standards for each variety are clearly and unambiguously laid down, together with the distribution of points. The total number of points awarded is 100 and these are divided into several sections.

In the long-haired varieties, the colour, marking and texture of coat are of paramount importance, and 40 to 50 points are given under these headings. The remaining points are devoted to the shape of the body and head, the tail, the shape and colour of eyes, etc.

In the British short-haired breeds, too, 50 points are given for body structure, coat and condition; the remaining 50 are for coat colour and eyes.

For the other short-haired cats the standards are similar, with especial attention paid to the individual peculiarities of each breed. 20 points, for example, are given under 'ticking' for Abyssinians; for Manx cats 15 points each are given for taillessness, height of hindquarters, and shortness of back, 10 for roundness of rump, and so on.

For the Seal-pointed Siamese, the shape of Body and Tail is defined as follows on the facing page:

'Dunloe Blue Cap', a Russian Blue cat, winner of First Prize in the 1954 All Breed Championship Show at Westminster.

56

Cream-coloured Persians in a Paris cat show.

Champion Long-haired Blue 'Paragon' shows his teeth.

Medium size, body long and svelte, legs proportionately slim, hind legs slightly higher than the front ones, feet small and oval, tail long and tapering (straight or slightly kinked at the extremity) . . .

The eyes must be 'Clear, brilliant deep blue. Shape Oriental and slanting towards the nose. No squint.' The Body Colour has to be 'Cream, shading gradually into pale warm fawn on the back.'

50 Points are awarded for Type and Shape, 50 for Colour, Coat Texture and Condition.

So if you happen to own a Seal-pointed Siamese with a kinky tail you may have a potential Champion, but if he has a squint you are probably wasting your time. Nor would it be any use entering a black cat with green eyes when the standard clearly calls for 'deep copper or orange with no trace of green.'

A prize-winning cat is a splendid animal, and for the breeder and owner it represents immeasurable value. For those whose pets can never hope to attain such giddy heights of fame, much useful information can be obtained and considerable pleasure derived from wandering round a show and seeing the peaks of perfection which patient care and experiment can achieve.

Although it is a thankless task at times, a debt of gratitude is surely due to all those who are concerned to see that breeding and exhibiting are subjected to constant scrutiny and supervision. In the long run it can result only in a steady improvement in standards and conditions, which in turn serves to promote the welfare of cats everywhere.

Monsignore Capecelatro and his Cats

I have observed, that all domestic animals are more amiable and intelligent on the continent than with us; it may be that they are better treated; for nothing tames like kindness. The fine breed of Angora cats, so common in the South of Italy, is a proof of the assertion; they are much caressed and attended to, and are as intelligent and as attachable as dogs. The first day we had the honour of dining at the palace of the Archbishop of Taranto, at Naples, he said to me, 'You must pardon my passion for cats (la mia passione gattesca), but I never exclude them from my dining-room, and you will find they make excellent company.'

Between the first and second course, the door opened, and several enormously large and beautiful cats were introduced, by the names of Pantalone, Desdemona, Otello, and other dramatic *cognomina*. They took their places on chairs near the table, and were as silent, as quiet, as motionless, and as well behaved, as the most bon ton table in London could require. On the Bishop requesting one of the chaplains to help the signora Desdemona to something, the butler stept up to his Lordship and observed, 'Desdemona will prefer waiting for the roast.' After dinner they were sent to walk on the terrace, and I had the honour of assisting at their coucher, for which a number of comfortable cushions were prepared in the bishop's dressing-room.

(Lady Morgan. *Book of the Boudoir*)

Who's for the beach?

Perfect balance

First steps

Cat and dog life

The Naming of Cats

The Naming of Cats is a difficult matter,
    It isn't just one of your holiday games;
You may think at first I'm as mad as a hatter
    When I tell you a cat must have THREE DIFFERENT NAMES.
First of all, there's the name that the family use daily,
    Such as Peter, Augustus, Alonzo or James,
Such as Victor or Jonathan, George or Bill Bailey –
    All of them sensible everyday names.
There are fancier names if you think they sound sweeter,
    Some for the gentlemen, some for the dames:
Such as Plato, Admetus, Electra, Demeter –
    But all of them sensible everyday names.
But I tell you, a cat needs a name that's particular,
    A name that's peculiar, and more dignified,
Else how can he keep up his tail perpendicular,
    Or spread out his whiskers, or cherish his pride?
Of names of this kind, I can give you a quorum,
    Such as Munkustrap, Quaxo or Coricopat,
Such as Bombalurina, or else Jellylorum –
    Names that never belong to more than one cat.
But above and beyond there's still one name left over,
    And that is the name that you never will guess;
The name that no human research can discover –
    BUT THE CAT HIMSELF KNOWS, and will never confess.
When you notice a cat in profound meditation,
    The reason, I tell you, is always the same:
His mind is engaged in a rapt contemplation
    Of the thought, of the thought, of the thought of his name:
    His ineffable effable
    Effanineffable
Deep and inscrutable singular Name.

(T. S. Eliot. *Old Possum's Book of Practical Cats*)

Some cats are fascinated by that screen.

Others just like to curl up under a table.

The Popularity of Cats

The first step

Assuming you have made up your mind to acquire a cat—a cat, mark you, not just a kitten, because that's what it is going to be for the best part of its life—how should you go about it? Probably few of your friends breed them, so the chances of your being given one are remote; nor are you likely just to find one, certainly not the one you have set your heart on. Resign yourself to the inevitable—you will have to buy one.

You will probably have a rough idea of the kind of cat you want, and what you want it for. If you are going in for breeding or exhibiting, you will do best to go to a well-known or personally recommended breeder. Along with the kitten you will receive a pedigree, but remember that for a pedigree cat you will have to pay that much more. Do not on any account be tempted by a 'bargain', or you may regret it later.

If you want a cat merely as a pet, and are not too particular about its background, go to a pet shop, but go to a good one. See that it is clean, well lit and well ventilated, and that the assistants really care about the animals in their keep. You can easily tell by the way they handle them and talk about them.

Whether buying from a breeder or a shop, be guided by the same general principles. Your final choice should be dictated partly by common sense and partly by instinct. Obviously you won't choose a kitten whose appearance and demeanour do not especially appeal to you. Probably you will fall for the one which responds eagerly to your approaches and seems to take to you. Watch it playing with the rest of its litter; ideally, it should be sociable and full of fun, but not wild. Test its reaction to your voice, bearing in mind that the majority of blue-eyed white kittens are born deaf.

Make sure, as far as you are able, that the kitten you select is in tip-top condition. You will have to take the assistant's word for anything the eye cannot detect, but you can make a rapid check of certain points. The kitten's eyes should be bright and its gaze alert, its ears should be clean, its tongue pink, its nose soft and moist. The fur should be glossy and the surface of the skin smooth to the touch, without any sings of sores and scabs. After purchasing, you should in any case have it examined by a veterinary surgeon.

Is anyone going to stand me a drink?

*Making doubly sure —
but the cat will take the credit!*

Male or female

Make up your mind beforehand whether you want a male or a female. This is a personal decision, and nobody can lay down rules on the matter. A female will probably turn out to be a more congenial companion, and if you want at least one litter your choice is automatic.

A male can be an equally affectionate pet, although you will probably decide to curb his roving and aggressive instincts by having him neutered. Remember, too, that a female can be spayed at any time, even after bearing her first litter. Both operations should be undertaken by qualified veterinary practitioners. There is little risk, no suffering, and no adverse effect on the cat's normal functions,

physique or character. Either operation may be carried out during the first six to eight months and most authorities say the earlier the better.

Before landing yourself with a cat make sure you have a good veterinary surgeon in the vicinity. A good vet is as essential as a good doctor is for you and your family. At some stage in your cat's life you are sure to need his services, even if only for routine checks. By all means arm yourself with a standard handbook on cat ailments and remedies, see that your medicine cupboard is well stocked and that you have an adequate first-aid kit. In this way you will be able to cope with most minor ailments and mishaps. But where there is the slightest doubt, the merest risk of something serious, certainly in case of accidents when broken bones may

The tabby and the Christmas tree.

A fellow can have the most awful nightmares –

– but when he wakes up to find it's true –

– the situation can sometimes be turned to good account.

Valuable stuff this, but I've never been known to break anything – yet.

A couple of connoisseurs pronounce their verdict.

be involved, consult your vet without hesitation. 'Do it yourself' may be dangerous if carried too far.

The new home

Take your new kitten home in a comfortable box or basket, and give it a good deal of love and attention during the first few days. You won't need to dovote a tremendous amount of time to it because it will need plenty of sleep, but it must have time to get accustomed to its new surroundings and to unfamiliar faces.

So don't expect it to be completely independent right away. Cats do not cling, and it will soon be fending for itself. But at first it may feel lonely and even insist on sleeping in your room or on your bed, in which case you should give way. See that it has a comfortable and warm sleeping place, not necessarily an elaborate bed of cushions and feathers, for an ordinary basket, box or carton will suffice, lined with a blanket or with newspaper. What is important is to ensure that the bed is in a sheltered position, well away from draughts. An even temperature is essential at any stage of a cat's life, for colds more often result from draughts than from cold and wet weather.

Food and drink

Find out from the breeder or pet shop as much as you can about your cat's previous diet and habits, and try to avoid any abrupt alteration in routine. If the kitten is ten weeks old or thereabouts, stick to fairly simple food for the first few weeks. Make sure it drinks plenty of water, and feed it often but in small quantities. As it grows it will need fewer and less regular meals, but larger portions. Its diet will become more varied, but it must always be properly balanced. Cats need proteins, carbohydrates, fats and minerals just as we do, though in different proportions, and they also need the proper vitamins to ensure steady growth and development.

Meat and fish are the cat's favourite staple dishes. However fastidious it may be, a cat will rarely refuse fish or meat altogether. It will probably enjoy either raw or cooked meat, and beef, lamb, offal, horsemeat, rabbit and poultry are all acceptable. Rabbit or poultry should be given sparingly and carefully boned; liver should also form only an occasional treat. Pork, which is rather fatty, may be dispensed with completely. Fish should always be cooked and all bones removed; any of the cheaper varieties of white fish are ideal.

These main dishes should be supplemented by vegetables, especially green ones such as spinach, but here the choice will depend largely on your cat's fads and fancies. Some like peas, some corn, others potatoes or tomatoes. None are harmful. Egg yolks are appreciated, but not too often. Biscuits, cereals and yeast are excellent, the last being valuable in vitamin content and available in tablet form.

Sometimes you can have too much cheese!

Peta, the Home Office cat, comes from the Isle of Man. Her wages are 5/- a week.

As for drinking, water should be on hand at all times, as it is by far the most refreshing and important drink for a cat. Kittens should also be given plenty of milk, but adult cats do not need either milk or cream in large quantities. In fact, some cats refuse to go near a saucer of milk. When you do give milk, however, always warm it slightly.

To make certain your kitten gets all the right vitamins, you should also include fish oils like halibut or cod-liver oil. They seem to take to them as naturally as babies. Finally, make sure your cat has access to grass, which is particularly valuable; it contains vitamins and aids the digestive functions. If you have no garden you can grow it in pots. Cocksfoot is the best variety.

Tinned foods are useful if you are pressed for time, and there are a number of excellent prepared cat foods on the market. But no cat-lover would dream of using tinned foods all the time. All cats appreciate and insist upon variety.

Doubtless your cat will have other more expensive and exotic fancies in the food line, and it would be foolish to deny it the occasional fling. It may be cake, fruit, nuts, shellfish, spaghetti, asparagus or ice-cream. Whatever it is do not be afraid of indulging it now and then, but refrain from making a habit of slipping it tit-bits at every meal, for overfeeding may have harmful effects. It is better to stick to the staple health-giving foods, with the odd delicacy thrown in, than to stuff it with an over-rich diet which may make

it grow fat and indolent. It is largely a matter of common sense and experiment. Your cat will soon show its disdain for food which is not to its liking or improperly prepared.

Keeping it clean

Cats are notoriously independent, self-sufficient animals, but in certain matters concerning health and hygiene, particularly when they are young, they may need assistance. You may be lucky enough to find your kitten already toilet-trained when you buy it, but the chances are it will need some simple guidance. So a sanitary tray should be provided within easy reach and in a fixed place. It can be lined with newspaper or dry earth, and must of course be regularly emptied and cleaned. The kitten will soon get the idea

Then there is the care of its coat. Cats are fastidiously clean and attend to their own basic washing and brushing up. But they do need help to keep their fur in prime condition, so it is advisable to brush and comb them at least once daily, and with Persians, twice a day. A bristle brush and combs with rounded teeth should be used, and you should be extra careful when the coat is badly matted or tangled, or when the cat is moulting, which is at least once a year.

At the same time, you should keep an eye on the cat's general condition. There are a number of

This object looks interesting.

I'll get someone for this!

harmless but irritating parasites which must be kept at bay—fleas, ticks and lice—all of which can be destroyed with powders; and it is vital to see that the eyes, ears and nose are all kept clean. There are many first-class manuals for the cat-owner, one or two of which (but preferably not more) should form part of your library.

Cats, on the whole, do not take kindly to being washed, though many are fascinated by dripping or running taps. It is not really necessary to give a cat a bath unless it is hopelessly dirty, but if you do, use only lukewarm water, keep the soap away from its eyes and dry the coat thoroughly when you have finished.

A study in contentment.

Travelling in comfort.

Mlle de Roma's 47 cats have completely taken over her little two room flat in Montmartre.

*Reaching
for the moon.*

Playtime

Kittens are by nature playful and mischievous, and whilst perfectly capable of amusing themselves and one another, they do like being entertained. The simplest playthings can amuse them for hours —ping-pong balls, cotton reels, catnip mice, scraps of paper, bits of string, pieces of felt-anything, in fact, which they can roll or pounce upon. Painted toys should, however, be avoided, as should anything which might have harmful effects if licked or swallowed.

Their adventurous instincts may also lead to their jumping up on furniture or scratching chair and table legs. Such innocent activities may well exasperate you, but try to keep your temper under control. Do not try to punish a cat as you would

Suppose it's raining again today.

Wonder of wonders, the sun's out.

a child. Smacks, going without dinner and solitary confinement are quite useless and meaningless to a cat. Of course such experiments must be discouraged or your house will be set all topsy-turvy. Try, in the first place, a firm but gentle verbal rebuke, followed if need be by a tap on the rump with a folded paper. Cats learn the meaning of 'no' without much difficulty. As for scratching, which is a natural form of exercise for a cat, the best solution is a scratching post or piece of wood on which it can wreak all the damage it desires. It is not sharpening its claws, but just keeping them clean and in condition.

Don't delude yourself that you can turn your cat into a wholly docile and obedient pet. Some of the things it does may not fill you with glee, but they are quite natural to the cat, and no amount of rebuke or punishment is going to have the slight-est effect. The cat does not have a human sense of right and wrong, and neither stealing food nor stalking birds seem especially evil in its eyes. You may achieve a limited amount of success, but if a cat does not chase birds it is either because a bird once gave him a sharp but unforgettable lesson, or you just happen to possess a cat who does not care a jot for that type of sport.

It is the same with mice. Nobody can prevent a cat from catching a mouse if it is so inclined. After all, they are not cuddly pets and it is pointless being sentimental about them. Laying a dead mouse or, worse still, a half-dead mouse at your feet may be your cat's way of paying you a supreme compliment. If you are really bothered about it you can only hope to get a cat which is genuinely good for mice, namely the one who leaves them alone. They also exist.

Not a cloud in the sky, either.

Might as well venture out then.

Bet you I finish first!

Cod liver oil also seems to go down well with most cats.

Two's company

It may be that your kitten will also need protection, especially where there are children around, or when another cat or different kind of animal already holds sway in the household. Children of course adore kittens, and it is fine for them to grow up together. They also seem to get away with murder, for kittens put up with undignified treatment by children which they would never take meekly from an adult. Both children and cats usually escape unscathed from these violent encounters, but all children should be told what not to do, such as pulling their tails and whiskers, picking them up too roughly by the scruff of their necks, administering sudden shocks and similar well-meant devilries.

Then there are the other established household pets. Provided they are introduced to each other gradually, there is no reason why a staunch friendship should not result. There may be a few initial squabbles, scratches, paw-cuffs and nips, but experience shows that a cat and a dog, to take the most obvious example, will soon settle down, sleeping, feeding and playing together, and soon becoming inseparable friends. They respect one another's rights, which after all are not that much at variance.

It may sometimes be more difficult to reconcile two cats. The new arrival can receive rough treatment at first, so, as with children, it is essential to give extra comfort and attention to the one who was there in the first place. Again, if the introduction is unforced and gradual, there should soon be concord and companionship. It has been said many times, but quite rightly, that the best plaything for a cat is another cat.

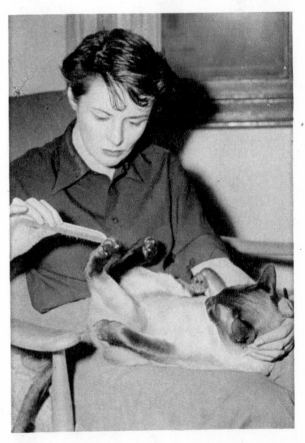

Most cats enjoy their daily grooming, and this Siamese is no exception.

75

Reaching for the bird.

Warm friends — the Blue Persian's name, Caesar, the parrot's, Cleopatra.

How did I come to be hanging up here?

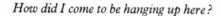

Water's all right as long as you can keep your face dry.

Film star Mickey Rooney and pet.

Out and about

Cats need plenty of fresh air and exercise as they grow, and if you have a garden you will have no worries. If you don't, you must still allow it out whenever it so desires, and if you are worried about losing it, provide it with a collar, an elastic not a leather one, which fits loosely around the neck. Cats can be trained to walk on a lead, but it should not prove necessary. It will probably embarrass you rather than your cat.

In general, your cat will neither require nor condone supervision, and will come and go as it pleases. It knows quite well when it needs exercise and when rest. It is as well to try to encourage it to stay in at night, especially in town. If it is well fed and comfortable it will certainly not venture out in bad weather, but as for amatory expeditions—try to stop these if you dare.

Sooner or later you will come up against the problem of holidays and travelling. Most cats welcome a change of surroundings, and provided you carry it in a cosy travelling basket and attend to its normal needs, you will probably have little

A good, long drink and then goldfish for supper I hope.

This way you can be sure of not being answered back.

trouble. Some cats, however, hate all forms of travel, and if yours is one of these, do not attempt to take it with you.

Anyway, it is not always convenient to take a cat on holiday. If you leave it at home, see that it can get in and out of its customary window, and make sure that a neighbour feeds it regularly. If your neighbours are particularly obliging they may house your cat for you, but such a change of routine can be upsetting. The other possibility is to leave it at one of the numerous boarding establishments, either privately run or under the control of one of the animal societies. At the best of these you may be sure that your cat will receive the utmost care and attention.

Moving house is not really a serious problem, provided you allow the cat to explore its new surroundings gradually, and make sure that it does not slip out unnoticed to try to make its way back to its former home. If it is obviously unsettled by the move, try the time-tested method of buttering the paws.

Keeping a cat involves a certain amount of time and trouble, that is obvious, and if you do not want to be bothered, then don't buy a cat in the first place. They need much less care than dogs, but they do expect companionship, affection, understanding, and a common-sense approach to their needs and problems. Do not pamper or overindulge them, but treat them with restraint and intelligence. The relationship will be close and infinitely rewarding.

A piece of string and it makes two happy.

*Safest place
is up a tree.*

*I'm meeting
that face all the
time, and I still
can't figure
it out.*

Snowy aristocrat

Artist's life

Knit one, purr one

Basketful of mischief

Lighter than air

True or False?

See how well you know your cats by trying to answer the following simple statements of facts correctly. The answers will be found at the back of the book, on page 152.

1. Some cats have lived more than thirty years.
2. Manx cats are expert climbers.
3. Sight is the last of the cat's senses to develop.
4. A falling cat always lands on its feet.
5. Abyssinian cats originally came from Abyssinia.
6. Dick Whittington and his cat really existed.
7. 'Mao' is a Chinese word for cat.
8. The colour of a kitten's eyes changes as it grows older.
9. An adult cat has thirty-two teeth.
10. A female cat may be physically mature at eight or nine months.
11. Raw meat is good for cats.
12. The Danes introduced the domestic cat into England.
13. The short-haired Blue Cream is not an officially recognised breed in Britain.
14. The long-haired Blue Cream is not an officially recognised breed in Britain.
15. The Havana cat was introduced to Britain from the United States in 1952.
16. Some cats have six toes on their fore feet.
17. There are only four wild cats in captivity in Britain.
18. The cheetah is the only type of wild cat which does not possess retractable claws.
19. The colocollo is a South American wild cat.
20. The colobus is an African wild cat.

How to Fall
on your Feet

*These pictures show a kitten
being dropped from a height
of two feet. During the short time
it takes to fall, the kitten
adroitly twists itself completely round
and comes down to a perfect
four-point landing.*

◀ *Pet in a pail.*

The Cat Will Survive

. . . But the cat will survive. He is no such fool as man. He knows that he must have Nature behind him. He also knows that it is easier for one cat alone to fit into the curves of Nature than two cats. So he walks by himself. For Nature here and Nature there are two different Natures and what one cat on one side of the fence has to do is not what another cat on the other side of the fence has to do. But the great principles are obeyed by all cats to such an extent that twenty, a hundred, a thousand cats will willingly give their lives, which they might easily save, to preserve an instinct, a racial memory, which will serve to perpetuate the feline race. The result will be that, after the cataclysm, out of the mounds of heaped-up earth, the piles and wrecks of half-buried cities, the desolated fields of grain, and the tortured orchards, the cat will stalk, confident, self-reliant, capable, imperturbable, and philosophical. He will bridge the gap until man appears again and then he will sit on new hearths and again will teach his mighty lesson to ears and eyes that again are dumb and blind. Shylock's doom was foretold by Shakespeare from the moment the poet asked the poor creature to say, 'the harmless necessary cat'. For it is possible, nay probable, that the cat, unlike man who forgets his previous forms, remembers, really remembers, many generations back; that what we call instinct may be more profound than knowledge. And so Providence wisely has not allowed the cat to speak any language save his own.

(Carl Van Vechten. *Tiger in the House*)

The Playtime of Cats

A kitten meets a toad.

Watch that weight!
Buttons and bows.

A bird in the claw . . .
Looking for a fight?

A ball of string is just made
to be unravelled.

Looking on the bright side of life.

'Curly Cat' kittens, bred on the Cornish moors.

The new generation

One of the most extraordinary cat stories, no less astonishing for the number of times it has been recounted, is that of the female cat who was accidentally imprisoned inside a packing case for motor parts in Detroit, U.S.A. The case was prised open six weeks later in Egypt, and the cat was found alive, though pathetically weak, having in the meantime given birth to a healthy litter of four kittens. The entire family had survived in complete darkness without food or water. In some miraculous way, the mother had fed her young and kept them alive during the terrifying ordeal.

This is an extreme instance of the cat's amazing powers of endurance and survival, but every owner of a cat can probably contribute similar, if less dramatic accounts of a female cat's adaptability and self-reliance in relation to her kittens. The process of giving birth is for her an intensely private affair, and it is indeed rare for her to require or demand human interference and assistance.

The gestation period of the cat is on average 63 days, and the actual birth takes about two hours, varying according to the physical condition of the mother and the size of the litter. Yet although she will go about it with the least amount of fuss, it is of course just as well to be hovering around in case anything goes wrong. You should, in any event, provide a box with soft bedding material, placed in a quiet spot away from draughts. The chances are she will give birth in a secluded corner of her own choosing, perhaps a shelf, a cupboard or wardrobe. Nor may she even take advantage of the bed later, but have it ready just in case.

If she is having obvious difficulty with the first kitten you may have to lend a hand, and should there be no sign of a kitten an hour or two after the commencement of labour, you may be obliged to call a veterinary surgeon. Such emergencies, however, are rare, and most cats produce their young with comparatively little bother or discomfort.

Each kitten is born in a separate sac, which is generally broken open at the moment of birth; if not, the mother bites it open. She also severs the umbilical cord and swallows the placenta. This is a perfectly normal phenomenon. The kittens are born completely blind, and the first thing the mother does is to lick them clean, this action also helping to stimulate their circulation. All you need do at this stage is to see that they are all warm and comfortable, leaving a saucer of water close at hand.

Provided that the mother has a normal supply of milk and that she possesses the usual healthy maternal instincts, no special attention will be required from you for ten days or so, apart from providing the necessary rations of food and drink, and keeping the bedding material clean. But should she be unable for any reason to feed the kittens herself, or should she be one of those mothers who is by nature neglectful of her duties, you may have to look for a foster mother or even raise the litter yourself by hand. This is a complicated business for which you will need expert advice. It involves, among other things, feeding the kittens regularly every two hours, day and night, for at least the first week. It is something which happens seldom, but the possibility should be borne in mind.

A laundry basket is this kitten's vantage point.

Kittens on the keys.

This is only one way of getting milk out of a bottle.

89

Home, James!

This cat gave birth to her kittens at the top of a chestnut tree.

A litter of Siamese Seal Point kittens.

Early days

Kittens at birth are neither distinctive nor beautiful, and if you are concerned about breeding true you may at first be confused and disappointed. But of course the markings of a newly-born kitten are highly deceptive, and many varieties do not acquire their normal coat colours and markings for many weeks. Siamese kittens, for example, are born white, Blue Persians have tabby markings, Black Persians are brown, and so on. A pedigree cat is very difficult to identify at birth.

In all probability, however, you will not be too worried about pedigrees, and a chance mating may result in a delightfully mixed litter. More important than the colour of a kitten's coat is the determination of its sex. Kittens should be sexed as soon as possible after birth, in fact as soon as the mother will permit them to be handled. Sexing kittens is not difficult, and the Cats' Protection League issues a useful set of diagrams for owners who may be in doubt.

Any unwanted kittens should be removed immediately after birth and handed over either to a competent veterinary surgeon or to one of the humane societies. These will either find a home for them or have them painlessly destroyed. Do not hang on to an entire litter out of fancied consideration for the mother; she will hardly notice the disappearance of two or three of her litter and much needless suffering can be avoided by taking this step without delay. If you decide to keep only one kitten, choose a male for preference.

By about the third day, the kittens, who until now have been aware of their surroundings only by touch, begin to develop their senses of smell and taste. A few days later they start responding to sounds, and at about ten days their eyes begin to open. During this period, when they are gradually becoming accustomed to novel sensations of light and shade, they should be confined in a darkened place.

Some days later they start trying to move about, teetering unsteadily and precariously on their spindly legs, but already showing clear signs of that independent and adventurous spirit which will characterise their lives as adult cats. The mother, meantime, endures all this bustling activity with remarkable coolness, occasionally joining in the game, giving them elementary lessons in mousing and now and then cuffing them back into line.

I don't care for music, actually. I just go for the ride.

We three.

Tabby relaxing.

Fiddling with string.

Mother and baby share a meal.

Adults in miniature

This is the time for you to assist the mother in getting the kittens house-trained and weaned. Normally she should have sufficient milk for about eight weeks, but by now they need a supplementary supply of food. You can easily get a kitten accustomed to the taste of warm milk by simply moistening its lips, and very soon you will have it lapping happily from a saucer. Milk is very important for a growing kitten and is one of the foods which you should insist upon giving it.

Go fairly easy on solid foods, for at this stage it is particularly risky to overfeed. Get it started gradually, and in small amounts, on raw minced meat, raw eggs, chopped poultry or rabbit, boiled fish and soft cereals. Any of the standard handbooks will give sensible advice on feeding. They will not necessarily agree in every detail, but they will certainly advise you on what to avoid. This may at first appear a bit silly, but if you fix firmly in your mind those foods which could be harmful to kittens, you are on pretty safe ground, and meticulously precise amounts and proportions do not matter too much.

At eight weeks the kitten should be getting at least four small meals a day. Then as it grows you can cut down on the meals and increase the portions. As the baby teeth appear you will no longer find it necessary to chop up the food so finely, and you can experiment with new types of food and thus arrive at a menu which is varied and palatable. By now the kittens are quite steady on their feet, and at their most appealing and delightful stage of development. They are full of fun and zest, with those wistful and half-surprised expressions which even manage to melt the hearts of people normally indifferent to cats.

Eight weeks is the age when the kittens may safely be removed from their mother, who has thus far fed them, trained them, cleaned them and played with them. Now they are ready to fend for themselves, and every day sees them become more energetic and mischievous. Very soon the mother, if you have decided to permit it, will be ready to begin the whole process over again, and will have little time to spare for her rapidly growing offspring. The kittens pass through a rather gawky, ungainly stage at three months, and at five shed their baby fur and take on a coarser permanent coat. At eight months the female kitten is already a mature cat, the male becoming a full adult only a few months later. Babyhood, for cats, lasts only a very short time.

Tobias really prefers to drink through a straw.

Kitten in the spokes.

Getting up was easy, but how do I get down?

Sentiment and sense

It is so easy, and by no means shameful, to be sentimental about kittens. They are entrancing creatures and a boundless source of joy and amusement. But it is cruel and dangerous to permit sentiment to override common sense. A cat is by nature capable of bearing up to three litters each year, with four to eight kittens in each litter. If only half the kittens are females, they will in turn be capable of producing their first litter within a year of their birth.

It does not need a great mathematical brain to demonstrate that the regulation of the cat population cannot be left to nature alone. That is why the disposal of unwanted kittens and the simple operations on both male and female adult cats are so necessary from the practical and humane points of view. One kitten, adequately and affectionately cared for, is surely better than six homeless, neglected ones; and anyone who keeps kittens must assume the responsibility for their growing into healthy and contented cats.

Human nature being what it is, the words of the poetess Joanna Baillie have a disturbing ring of truth about them. In her poem *The Kitten,* after describing the delightful antics of the kitten, and the applause and affection which surround it, she begins the final verse as follows:—

And so, poor kit! must thou endure,
When thou becom'st a cat demure,
Full many a cuff and angry word,
Chased roughly from the tempting board.
But yet, for that thou hast, I ween,
So oft our favour'd play-mate been,
Soft be the change which thou shalt prove! . . .

It is up to us to make absolutely certain that the 'favour'd play-mate' grows up to become an equally favoured companion and friend.

An orderly queue might be easier in the long run.

It's that mirror again.

All zipped up, but nowhere to go.

The Fireside Sphinx

Half loving-kindliness and half disdain,
   Thou comest to my call serenely suave,
With humming speech and gracious gestures grave,
   In salutation courtly and urbane:

Yet must I humble me thy grace to gain –
   For wiles may win thee, but no arts enslave,
   And nowhere gladly thou abidest save
Where naught disturbs the concord of thy reign.

Sphinx of my quiet hearth! who deignst to dwell
   Friend of my toil, companion of mine ease,
   Thine is the lore of Ra and Rameses;
That men forget dost thou remember well,
   Beholden still in blinking reveries,
   With sombre sea-green gaze inscrutable.

(Graham R. Tomson)

Persians

Persian cats, with their soft, flowing silky hair are obviously built for comfort, not for speed, and the best specimens are unsurpassed for sheer beauty. The longer and softer the coat, the better the cat; and the better the cat, the more trouble has to be taken in keeping the coat clean and in good condition.

A Persian in repose looks the most indolent creature alive, but it needs fresh air and exercise just like any other cat, and can hunt, climb and play along with the most energetic of its short-haired cousins. But whether or not it is because of that extra bit of care which is lavished on them, they are in general better-behaved and more contented than most other cats.

A selection of Persians of all sizes and hues, behaving for the most part, like Persians.

Kangaroo inspects kitten.

The Kitten and the Kangaroo

Kitten outstares kangaroo.

Kitten grabs kangaroo.

Kitten embraces kangaroo.

Kangaroo accepts kitten.

Matthias and Atossa

Poor Matthias! Would'st thou have
More than pity? claim'st a stave!
—Friends more near us than a bird
We dismissed without a word,
Rover, with the good brown head,
Great Atossa, they are dead;
Dead, and neither prose nor rhyme
Tells the praises of their prime.
Thou did'st know them old and grey,
Knew them in their sad decay.
Thou hast seen Atossa sage

Sit for hours beside thy cage;
Thou would'st chirp, thou foolish bird,
Flutter, chirp—she never stirr'd!
What were now these toys to her?
Down she sank amid her fur;
Eyed thee with a soul resign'd—
And thou deemedst cats were kind!
—Cruel, but composed and bland,
Dumb, inscrutable and grand,
So Tiberius might have sat,
Had Tiberius been a cat.

(Matthew Arnold. *Poor Matthias*)

Pampas Cat – very savage.

White cat — only pretends to be.

The Precursors of Cats

Looking for an ancestor

It seems only fitting that so little should be known about the origins of the ordinary domestic cat. Despite the abundance of ingenious theories, some based on genuine scientific observation, others on little more than inspired guesswork, the fact remains that scarcely anything is reliably known about the cat's ancestry.

The evolution of the horse has been convincingly traced back to the period when mammals first made their appearance on earth. There is a clear line of development from *Eohippus* with his four toes on the fore feet and three on the hind feet, down to *Equus* with his single toes back and front. There are slight differences in size and bone structure but it is undeniably the same creature.

How convenient it would be, therefore, to prove that the gentle tabby is the direct descendant of the savage European wild cat, who, according to fossil remains, has prowled the forests for millions of years. The wild cat still exists, though its numbers are fast dwindling. In Britain it is now confined to the Scottish Highlands. In physical structure and colouration, if not in temperament, it closely resembles our short-haired varieties. It would be tempting to link the two directly in the chain of evolution, but unfortunately this is one point on which all the experts agree. Although our domestic breeds undoubtedly have wild blood in

their veins, they are emphatically not descended from the European wild cats.

Considering that our cats have only been tame for a few thousand years, it is hardly surprising that they retain many of the instincts and characteristics of their jungle relatives. Even the mildest tabbies or the most sedate Persians can transform themselves into hissing and snarling furies if beset by danger. Like their wild cousins they are solitary, nocturnal creatures, enormously self-reliant and adaptable, marvels of muscular energy and flexibility. Their powers of perception seem to have been blunted very little by civilised surroundings.

Physically, the domestic cats differ very little from leopards, jaguars and ocelots—bone structure, teeth formation, fur, whiskers, eyes, pads, retractable claws, are the same. Watch a cat stalking a bird as silently and relentlessly as a tiger stalking an antelope; see the most ordinary household pet climbing a tree with the assurance and agility of a leopard; observe a mother fiercely guarding her new-born litter against a sudden intruder—a lioness could not be more jealous and determined. True, selective breeding in recent years has produced a range of coat colours and markings which are unknown and unnecessary in the jungle or on the pampas; but they are still members of the genus *Felidae*, and somewhere back in the remote past, the parent of them all made its lair in the caves or in the undergrowth.

Jungle Cat of North Africa, Central Asia and Southern Asia.

Pallas's Cat, resident of Central Asia.

Leopard taking his ease.

American Cougar or Mountain Lion.

Fifty million years back

It is now generally thought that this common ancestor was a weasel-like creature called Miacis, who roamed the plains and forests more than fifty million years ago. Miacis did not much look like the cats we know today, and probably bore a closer resemblance to the modern civets and genets. These animals are really carnivorous creatures, common to Africa and Asia, but they have some physical features which resemble those of the cat tribe, so it is not mere fancy to try to link them in prehistoric times. If Miacis is accepted as the starting point, it is likely that he is the ancestor not only of the cat tribe but also of the dogs, bears, civets and raccoons.

Nevertheless, innumerable missing links, extinct species and interbreedings make it impossible to trace any clear line of development from Miacis. One branch which certainly became extinct was the sabre-toothed clan. The sabre-toothed cat was probably as large and powerful as the modern lion, but in the end its enormously enlarged front teeth became a handicap rather than an asset in the quest for food. The less massive, but better adapted members of the family survived, and from this branch the true cats descended.

So there is a huge veil of silence and mystery covering the millions of years separating the sabre-toothed cats and the jungle-dwellers of today. There is not a trace of a cat in cave-drawings, nor have any fossils been dug up in the vicinity of prehistoric sites. There is nothing, in fact, to prepare us for the sudden emergence of the cat as the friend and companion of man in Egypt more than four thousand years ago.

Geoffroy's Cat, from
South America.

Scottish Wild Cat.

African Wild Cat or Kaffir Cat.

Caracal.

They may have had a common ancestor.

Eyra Cat.

Puma cub.

The elusive family tree

Where the tame cat sprang from, or exactly when and how other varieties emerged, we do not know. It is assumed that the Egyptian sacred cat was a domesticated African wild cat, and that the European domestic short-haired cats were similarly descended. The Egyptian or Caffre Cat still roams wild in Africa. It has a yellowish coat with faint stripes, dark horizontal bands on the limbs, and a long, ringed, black-tipped tail. It is also known to breed with domestic cats. So here is a strong probability, but no conclusive evidence; and although it may explain where the striped cats came from, it does not help with the blotched ones.

Even the true origin of the Siamese cat has not been satisfactorily established. The so-called Temple Cat was being exported from Siam in the nineteenth century, but it may just as well have had African rather than Asiatic ancestors. As for the enigmatic Manx cat, it is possible that he may have swum ashore from the shipwrecked vessels of the Spanish Armada and settled in the Isle of Man. But to upset this theory is the fact that cats with no tails also flourish in parts of Russia, and that several short-tailed varieties are known in the East. So perhaps we ought to seek the parents of the Manx cat in that part of the world.

When we come to the long-haired varieties, similar uncertainty prevails, though the possible geographical limits have been somewhat narrowed.

Probably the Angoras, or Persians, as they are now called, did not travel such vast distances during their long and gradual development. Many experts claim that their common ancestor is a creature of the central Asiatic plains and deserts, the Manul or Pallas's Cat. This is a small-sized animal with long soft fur, a short bushy tail, and a broad flattened head. Other authorities, however, deny this relationship, and point out that long hair is not necessarily associated only with cold regions. So here too the battle rages fiercely.

It is really futile to try to trace each and every breed back to a wild ancestor. New breeds occur, quite unexpectedly, because of changes in the sexual cells. It is to biology, therefore, rather than to geography that we should look. Every breeder knows how much trial and error is involved in attempting to produce pure strains. Even when the stock is supposedly pure on both sides, there may be surprises in store when the litters appear.

The modern cat does not much resemble Miacis; and merely because he possesses the agility of the puma, the gait of the tiger, the acceleration of the cheetah, the climbing power of the leopard and the temper of the jungle cat, does not in itself prove or disprove his descent from any one species. The research will go on, the theories will continue to fascinate and tantalise, the Latin names will be tossed around with glee and abandon. Yet some of us will devoutly hope that the cat will long be permitted to retain its oldest and most basic secret.

Lions, kings of the cat world.

Abyssinian cat, strong but gentle.

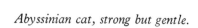

The cat guards his secret.

Dr Johnson and his Cat, Hodge

Nor would it be just under this head, to omit the fondness which he shewed for animals which he had taken under his protection. I never shall forget the indulgence with which he treated Hodge, his cat; for whom he himself used to go out and buy oysters, lest the servants having that trouble should take a dislike to the poor creature. I am, unluckily, one of those who have an antipathy to a cat, so that I am uneasy when in the room with one; and I own, I frequently suffered a good deal from the presence of the same Hodge. I recollect him one day scrambling up Dr Johnson's breast, apparently with much satisfaction, while my friend, smiling and half-whistling, rubbed down his back, and pulled him by the tail; and when I observed he was a fine cat, saying, 'Why, yes, Sir, but I have had cats whom I liked better than this'; and then, as if perceiving Hodge to be out of countenance, adding, 'but he is a very fine cat, a very fine cat indeed.'

This reminds me of the ludicrous account which he gave Mr Langton, of the despicable state of a young gentleman of good family. 'Sir, when I heard of him last, he was running about town, shooting cats.' And then, in a sort of kindly reverie, he bethought himself of his own favourite cat, and said, 'But Hodge shan't be shot: no, no, Hodge shall not be shot.'

(James Boswell. *Life of Samuel Johnson*)

Montaigne Plays with his Cat

... as the learned and ingenious Montaigne says like himself freely, 'When my cat and I entertain each other with mutual apish tricks, as playing with a garter, who knows but I make my cat more sport than she makes me? Shall I conclude her to be simple, that has her time to begin or refuse to play as freely as I myself have? Nay, who knows but that it is a defect of my not understanding her language (for doubtless cats talk and reason with one another) that we agree no better? And who knows but that she pities me for being no wiser than to play with her, and laughs and censures my folly for making sport for her, when we two play together?'

Thus freely speaks Montaigne concerning cats ...

(Izaak Walton. *The Compleat Angler*)

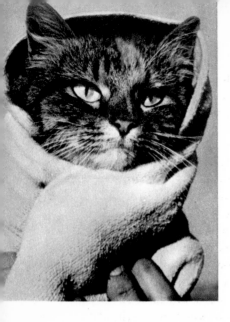

This cat had a miraculous escape from the casing of an electric train, in which it had been trapped for three days.

The P.D.S.A. found homes for these two adorable kittens.

The Protection of Cats

The right to live

'Prevention is better than cure' runs the old proverb, and it is as true of animals as it is of ourselves. The humane societies all over the world which devote themselves exclusively to the welfare of animals are well aware of this simple truth. It applies equally to the prevention of cruelty and the prevention of illness, and on both fronts steady advances are recorded as each year passes. But until brutality and disease vanish completely, there will be a crying need for cure as well as for prevention, and the welfare organisations have to fulfil both necessities.

The fight against disease and illness is a matter for scientific research; the fight against cruelty is a concern of humanity as a whole. Cruelty to animals is entirely man-made, and decent, humane treatment can be brought about only by persistent propaganda, education, and pressure of public opinion.

This arduous and, for the most part, ungrateful work continues all the time, though it is rarely sufficiently sensational to receive much publicity. In Britain, it began on an organised basis early in the nineteenth century, a period which saw a gradual but genuine improvement in the welfare of the less fortunate sections of the population. Political rights, working and housing conditions, female and child labour, education, hospitals—

there was so much to be done, all of it vital work, that it was hardly surprising if the welfare of animals should come fairly low on the national agenda.

Thanks to the enterprise and enthusiasm of certain individuals, the Royal Society for the Prevention of Cruelty to Animals was founded in 1824. Had it not been for the steady pressure brought to bear by this body upon successive ministries, it is doubtful whether any legislation would have been passed at all. As it was, five Acts relating to animals were passed between 1822 and 1854, and since then there has been a steady flow of legislation on the subject.

Today, every animal, whether pet or servant, is entitled to protection by law. True, there are still loopholes; too many instances where cruelty can go undetected and unpunished. In the opinion of some, the penalties for cruelty and negligence are still inadequate. Others maintain that animals receive more consideration than children in the eyes of the law.

The change in public attitude is, however, very marked. A century ago, a case of cruelty would hardly have merited more than local, passing attention. Nowadays, thanks largely to press publicity, it may arouse public opinion and public conscience on a national scale. We might almost say, though it sounds arrogant and a little cynical, that we are at last beginning to treat our animals like human beings.

Preventing cruelty

The Royal Society for the Prevention of Cruelty to Animals, which is the oldest animal protection society in the world, relies for its existence on public charity, as do the similar organisations which were formed later. This takes the form of subscriptions, donations and legacies. Although the public response is generous, there is, however, never enough money available for all the urgent work which has to be done.

The R.S.P.C.A., being mainly concerned with combating cruelty to animals in all guises, maintains a staff of inspectors over 200 strong, and the numerous cases of cruelty which they discover and investigate frequently lead to police prosecution, and sometimes to prison sentences.

Cats, of course, are only one of the many kinds of animals involved, but the instances of cruelty to cats are proportionately greater than for any other type of domestic animal. The methods of inflicting suffering seem more subtle and barbarous, and since the cat population is so vast, the opportunities are more numerous.

The maximum penalty for ill-treating a cat is £25 or up to three months' imprisonment. Negligence is also liable to a fine of up to £10, and on top of this may be added compensation to owners, plus costs. Abandoning a cat, according to recent legislation, is liable to similar penalties.

Statistics show that convictions for cruelty still run at a steady level, though the figures for the last two years record a slight decrease. In 1958, there were 90 convictions for cruelty to cats; in 1959, there were 66, with two offenders sent to prison. Some of the cases were quite horrifying—a cat

Just one of the many jobs the R.S.P.C.A. do. Shandy, a missing cat, was spotted on a roof top. An R.S.P.C.A. Inspector was soon on the spot undertaking a perilous rescue. Soon Shandy, realizing he had no head for heights, was brought down to earth, and returned to his master's arms.

The P.D.S.A. rescued this kitten from the fan belt of a lorry in which it was wedged. An X-ray showed it to be unharmed.

A cat's nine lives. This cat was heard yowling in the chimney of an apartment block in New York. The A.S.P.C.A. was called to the scene and managed to lasso the errant cat, which looks somewhat chastened by its adventure.

thrown by a sailor out of a ship at Birkenhead on to the dockside, a cat tossed by a labourer into the River Severn, and a ghastly case brought before a juvenile court involving two brothers, aged 13 and 16, who savagely killed two cats in a chaff-cutting machine. It is sobering to be confronted with such instances of wanton and unprovoked barbarity in this enlightened age. Unfortunately, they still happen only too often.

The R.S.P.C.A., in common with the other animal welfare societies in Britain, provides homes for unwanted cats, carries out humane destruction and neutering, runs animal clinics which dispense free treatment in needy cases, and operates boarding homes for animals temporarily deprived of their owners. It provides advice relating to animal care, issues a journal entitled *Animal World*, publishes pamphlets, arranges lectures and film-shows, and employs every national medium for educating the public in kindness to animals. Children from 7 to 16 years of age can join the Animal Defenders, and have their own magazine, *Animal Ways*. The Society also runs a hostel at London Airport for birds and animals in transit.

The other animal welfare societies in Britain are more concerned with care and cure than with law reform and prosecution. The Blue Cross Animal Welfare Society, which incorporates Our Dumb Friends League, was founded at the beginning of this century. It has branches all over Great Britain and boasts three splendidly equipped animal hospitals at Victoria and Hammersmith in London, and in Grimsby. It also maintains a modern mobile surgery in Dublin.

These hospitals provide the most up-to-date medical and surgical treatment, being fitted out with proper wards, surgeries, operating theatres, out-patients' dispensaries, X-ray units—in fact, the amenities of a modern hospital for humans.

The Blue Cross likewise runs clinics, shelters and homes for domestic animals. Owners of patients are expected to donate whatever they can afford towards the work of the Society. As far as cats are concerned, the Blue Cross deals in the usual manner with strays and unwanted pets. It also publishes an illustrated quarterly journal, *The Blue Cross Illustrated*.

The People's Dispensary for Sick Animals, established in 1917, also provides treatment absolutely free for animals belonging to those who cannot afford private veterinary consultation. It was, in fact, founded specifically for this purpose. Today the P.D.S.A. maintains 83 permanent dispensaries, 23 travelling dispensaries and five hospitals, of which the main one is at Ilford,

Essex. This is a finely equipped establishment, complete with in-patients' wards, isolation wards, operating theatre, out-patients' dispensary, and laboratory. It can handle any kind of surgical emergency, and these often include maternity cases. A fleet of 18 ambulances is in constant service.

Also at Ilford, in a quiet spot surrounded by meadows, is the Animal Cemetery, where several thousand graves of departed pets are tended with care and devotion.

The P.D.S.A. treats almost one million assorted cases annually, and in 1959 dealt with almost 200,000 cats, disposing humanely of nearly 80,000.

No less than 6,616 calls were received to rescue cats in chimneys and from other inaccessible places.

The P.D.S.A. also runs a children's group called the Busy Bee Movement, with its own journal, and a junior organisation called the Animal Service Guild, also with its own paper. There is, in addition, a constant stream of leaflets, and numerous lectures and film shows are given, calculated to promote the work of the Dispensary and to educate people in the care of their animals.

The Cats' Protection League, whose headquarters are in Slough, was founded in 1927, and differs from all the above-mentioned organisations in that it is

An emergency crew of the A.S.P.C.A., the American equivalent of the R.S.P.C.A., rescuing a cat from a piece of driftwood on which it had been floating down the river.

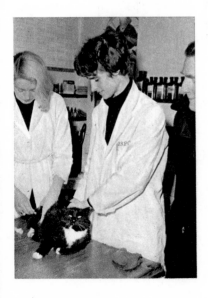

In an R.S.P.C.A. surgery an injection is given to a cat.

The R.S.P.C.A. special pet carrier.

Private enterprise in Naples, Italy. Signora Sidro runs a home for strays, and cares for over 150 cats of all breeds.

A cat being X-rayed at the R.S.P.C.A.

An official of the R.S.P.C.A. holds a cat which was found abandoned in a sack.

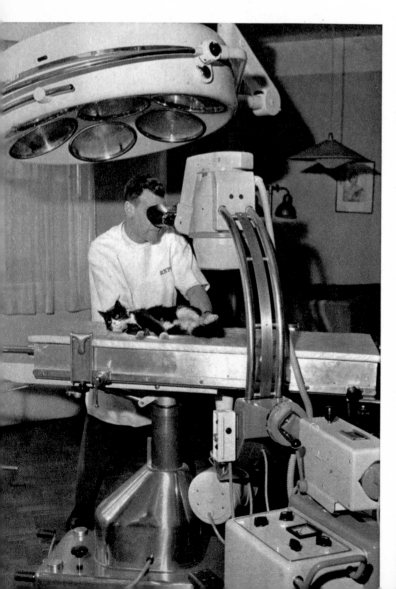

A passer-by found this cat by the roadside shut up in the box shown and took it to the police station. Here the cat is being cross-examined after his lucky escape.

This kitten with such an appealing expression was abandoned on a doorstep.

the only one devoted entirely to the welfare of cats. The League, too, spends much of its time finding homes for unwanted cats and kittens, and performs routine clinical work in addition to major surgical operations. The painful but necessary work of humane destruction is among the League's many functions.

The Cats' Protection League has branches in many parts of England and two in Ireland, and publishes a monthly magazine called *The Cat* which includes progress reports from all areas, letters, poems and anecdotes from members, book reviews, appeals and news items of interest to cat-lovers. The League also does a great deal of educational work, and issues a valuable series of leaflets dealing with every conceivable aspect of cat welfare and protection.

Many of the activities of these organisations necessarily overlap, but it is encouraging to learn that so many efficient societies now exist who are ready and equipped to deal with the ailments of cats and the many problems connected with their care. It is the proud boast of all these groups that animals deserve and receive the same high standard of treatment afforded to humans. Only qualified veterinary staff are employed, and for them it is absorbing and rewarding work.

Thanks, too, to the example of these humane societies the good work is carried on overseas by associated or affiliated groups—in all parts of the Commonwealth, in the Middle East, on the Continent, in North and South America. Methods vary, differences of opinion occur, competition sometimes replaces coordination, but all are fred with similar ideals and none are run to financial advantage.

Kindness to animals and to fellow human beings seem such obvious and simple aims, but too many people take them for granted and leave it to others to translate into practical terms. To those few who devote their working lives to such causes should go not only our thanks and warm wishes, but also our practical and material assistance.

Here A.S.P.C.A. men have to chisel out a couple of bricks to save a kitten. How it got there is anyone's guess.

Tortoiseshell–and–white

Fireside pose

Siamese arrogance

What cat's averse to fish?

Hogging the camera

Abyssinians

These rare cats, with their handsome 'ticked' coats may or may not be of sacred descent but their demeanour and appearance is certainly aristocratic and dignified. The coat colour should ideally be ruddy-brown and each hair may have two or three bands of colour, red, brown or black.

In repose they sometimes adopt a lion-like posture, and like most of the so-called Foreign short-haired cats, they are strong and courageous. In marked contrast to the Siamese, however, their voices are soft, almost meek and are very seldom used. They are playful, intelligent and companionable pets.

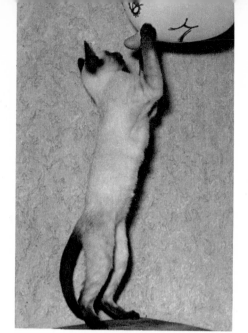

The Thing from Outer Space

On a Favourite Cat, Drowned in a Tub of Gold Fishes

'Twas on a lofty vase's side
Where China's gayest art had dyed
  The azure flowers that blow;
Demurest of the tabby kind,
The pensive Selima reclined,
  Gazed on the lake below.

Her conscious tail her joy declared;
The fair round face, the snowy beard,
  The velvet of her paws,
Her coat, that with the tortoise vies,
Her ears of jet, and emerald eyes,
  She saw; and purred applause.

Still had she gazed; but midst the tide
Two angel forms were seen to glide,
  The Genii of the stream:
Their scaly armour's Tyrian hue
Through richest purple to the view
  Betrayed a golden gleam.

The hapless Nymph with wonder saw:
A whisker first and then a claw,
  With many an ardent wish,
She stretched in vain to reach the prize
What female heart can gold despise?
  What Cat's averse to fish?

Presumptuous Maid! with looks intent
Again she stretched, again she bent,
  Nor knew the gulf between.
(Malignant Fate sat by, and smiled.)
The slipp'ry verge her feet beguiled,
  She tumbled headlong in.

Eight times emerging from the flood
She mewed to every watery god,
  Some speedy aid to send.
No Dolphin came, no Nereid stirred:
Nor cruel Tom, nor Susan heard.
  A Fav'rite has no friend!

From hence, ye Beauties, undeceived,
Know, one false step is ne'er retrieved,
  And be with caution bold.
Not all that tempts your wand'ring eyes
And heedless hearts is lawful prize;
  Nor all that glisters, gold.

(Thomas Gray)

A detail from The Return of Ulysses *by the Italian artist* Pinturicchio. *(National Gallery)*

The Portrayal of Cats

Grace and proportion

The portrayal of the cat in literature, music, painting and the plastic arts has tended to reflect its fortunes and misadventures throughout the course of history. When the cat's popularity has been at its summit, writers and painters have represented it as an animal full of elegance and wisdom. When its fortunes have sunk to a low ebb, not only the volume but also the inspiration of artistic effort has fallen to a similar level. A work of art must be exceptionally well-wrought from the technical point of view when the subject is drawn in unflattering guises; and when literature and art have attempted to bring out only the evil aspect of the cat, it must be admitted that from the creative point of view it has not added up to very much.

It is to Egypt that we must turn once more for the earliest works of art in which cats featured prominently. Most of the tomb paintings, many of which have been preserved in good condition, date from the 18th and 19th Dynasties, about 3,500 years ago. One drawing of a kitten watching its prey dates back almost 4,000 years.

The Egyptian paintings show various types of spotted or striped cats in their everyday surroundings. They are seated or curled up under chairs and thrones, nursing kittens, gnawing bones, playing with children and hiding among papyrus plants. That the Egyptians made good use of cats for hunting is shown by paintings of them pouncing on water-fowl and accompanying fishermen in their boats. The symbolic aspect is also powerfully depicted in the painting of the Great Cat Ra slaying the snake-dragon of darkness.

The magnificent bronze statues and statuettes of Bastet, the cat-headed goddess, and of cats in various attitudes, sometimes with kittens, are of a somewhat later period. Quite apart from their undoubted artistic merit, they show a vivid insight into the true character of the cat. The Egyptians also enjoyed representing their cats in miniature, on sistrums, bracelets, necklaces, brooches and other ornaments. We are left in no doubt, thanks to these artists and craftsmen, of the lofty position which the cat held in society.

But as the significance of the cat dwindled, so it came to be virtually neglected as a subject for artistic representation. Images of cats occasionally appear during the Roman period in mosaics or on vases, but they are rarely shaped with any great skill or perception; and the artists of the Orient seem to have ignored their existence completely, despite the fact that cats were household pets at an early date.

Ornaments from ancient Egypt. Two bracelet ends with cat figures. (British Museum)

Nebamun out hunting with his cat, who is seen pouncing on two water-fowl. This painting dates back three thousand years. (British Museum)

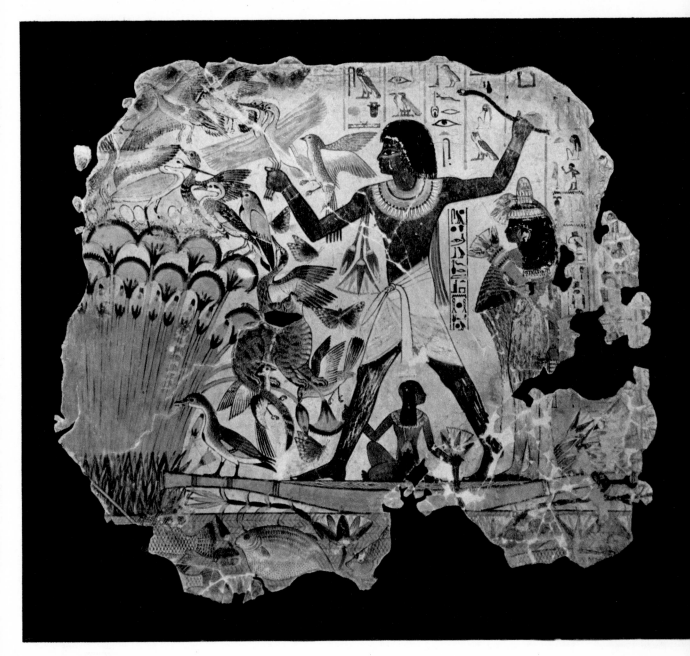

The Holy Family *by the Italian painter Baroccio. (National Gallery)*

A study of cats by Leonardo da Vinci. (Victoria and Albert Museum)

A harmless necessary cat

Writers, of course, continued to mention the cat, but casually, as a part of mere everyday existence. One exception, and the earliest mention of a domestic cat in British literature, is a poem entitled *Pangur Ban*. It was written by an Irish scholar and dates from the ninth century. The poet, and owner of the cat, tells how both pursue their own ways of life, one busy with his books, the other with his mice. He betrays a real fondness and appreciation of the cat's unique qualities.

This feeling is conspicuously lacking in the occasional references, some of them most disparaging, of many later and more celebrated writers. Chaucer, for example, in the *Manciple's Tale*, is merely content to point out that a cat, well nourished on milk and choicest meat, will forsake them all for a tasty mouse. And later still, Shakespeare, who never displayed any special fondness for domestic animals of any description, has only the most superficial things to say about them. To him it was little more than 'a harmless necessary cat'.

Pictures are also few and far between. There are several drawings of the renowned Sir Richard Whittington, thrice Lord Mayor of London, with his legendary cat. There is much doubt as to whether Whittington was quite such an ardent lover of cats as is commonly thought, but writers and artists have made them inseparable. It would be cruel to deprive successive generations of pantomime-lovers of their cherished illusions about Dick Whittington and his Cat.

There is one 16th century portrait of Sir Henry Wyat, a member of Henry VII's privy council. It shows him sitting in a prison cell—apparently he served a number of prison sentences—and next to him is his well-loved cat. This particular cat used to bring its master pigeons from outside, and the painting shows the cat dragging the bird through the bars of the cell.

Words and shapes

As the cat gradually crept back into popular favour after its temporary disgrace during the Middle Ages, so once again it became an apt subject for writers and artists of varying degrees of skill.

In the nineteenth century, particularly in France, torrents of prose and poetry gushed out in praise of the cat. Most of the eminent men who wrote sonnets and essays to their cats were passionately fond of them and understood the complexities of their natures. Mallarmé mentioned his cat Lilith in his letters; Baudelaire wrote three fine poems to cats; Taine wrote no less than twelve sonnets to his pets; Gautier wrote fondly and vividly of his cats in *La Ménagerie Intime;* Balzac, Zola and many others bring them frequently into the pages of their novels.

Girl with Kitten *by the French painter Perronneau. (National Gallery)*

Cat and Kittens – *a watercolour by Gottfried Mind. (Courtauld Institute of Art)*

Cat with Kittens – *a pen and wash drawing by Francis Barlow. (Courtauld Institute of Art)*

From that time on, the flood of literature swelled uncontrollably. There were poems, essays, memoirs, letters, scientific treatises, children's rhymes, satires—suddenly the cat had come into its own again. In the twentieth century, eminent writers such as Compton Mackenzie, Walter de la Mare, Hilaire Belloc, Carl van Vechten, Edith Sitwell, T. S. Eliot and countless others have celebrated cats, seriously and humorously, in poems, novels and short stories. Moreover, there is hardly an issue of a popular newspaper or magazine which does not carry a story or picture of a cat among its contributions.

In painting, too, the cat began to insinuate itself again after a long period of neglect. Leonardo da Vinci made several studies of cats, and a number of Italian, Flemish and Spanish painters included cats, generally for decorative purposes only. It was not until the eighteenth century that cats began being observed and painted for their own sakes.

In England, Hogarth often inserted in his engravings scrawny-looking cats in dubious surroundings. These lean and hungry animals appear in *A Rake's Progress, Industry and Idleness* and *The Four Stages of Cruelty*. In the 'First Stage of Cruelty', two unfortunate cats are shown being tortured by hanging upside-down from a lamp iron, whilst another is being tossed from an upstairs window, apparently in an effort to make it fly. But in his well-known painting *The Graham Children* Hogarth depicts a cat in more tender and congenial circumstances.

Other English artists who at one time or other painted cats included Barlow, the first native animal painter, Stubbs, the greatest animal artist of his age, and Morland, who treated his subject in a tender and perceptive manner. Stubbs, who was the most talented of the three, usually preferred wilder and more active animal subjects.

But it was during the nineteenth century, as in literature, that artists again began drawing and painting and modelling cats with genuine feeling and attention to detail. The French painters Delacroix and Géricault, though also attracted more by the wild and savage element of animal life, both portrayed domestic cats with care and warmth. In Japan, the greatest painter of his day, Hokusai, followed by several other lesser masters, used a full range of colours to depict cats in many moods and guises. Hokusai's cats are generally tailless, and all the Japanese artists see the cat as something more than a mere decorative pet. There is intense realism and, in addition, a touch of the supernatural in these attractive works of art.

In Switzerland, Gottfried Mind, the so-called

The Graham Children *by Hogarth. (Tate Gallery)*

'Raphael of Cats', had no other companions save his pet cats. He was one of the few artists whose works consist almost exclusively of drawings and paintings of his favourite animals. His art testifies to the years of patient observation and devotion which he brought to bear on his subjects. Another painter who enjoyed tremendous popularity for a time was Henriette Ronner. Her talent was slighter than Mind's, her cats being competently and prettily drawn, but showing little subtlety or marked personality.

In a category of his own was the artist Louis Wain, who at one time was turning out some 1500 drawings each year. Wain was essentially a caricaturist, and his rollicking, gambolling cats and kittens appeared in magazines, children's books, annuals and newspapers, on postcards, posters and calendars. Cats were depicted in every walk of life—human life, at any rate, for usually they were simply cat-like humans. They may not have possessed enormous artistic merit, but Wain certainly knew and adored cats, and was for a time a breeder and judge for the Cat Fancy. Louis Wain was for many years a household word, though today almost forgotten. He helped, in no small way, to popularise cats and to entertain young and old alike.

Today the camera has to a large extent replaced the artist's brush. The cat is one of the most widely photographed subjects, an overwhelming favourite for the manufacturers of chocolates and greetings cards. The really expert cat photographer needs a high degree of skill and limitless patience, for the cat is a notoriously difficult animal to pose. It needs a specialist to get the most striking results.

The cat has played its part—though not a very serious one—in the world of films, particularly in animated cartoons. Felix the Cat is little remembered nowadays but the Tom and Jerry cartoons and the appealing personality of Figaro in Disney's *Pinocchio* have made their enduring impression on children everywhere.

127

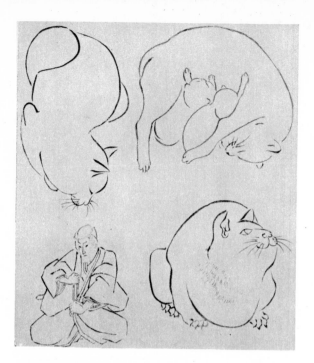

Music and dance

Many musicians have been fond of cats, but expressing their admiration of their pets in musical terms is not a particularly rewarding occupation. Domenico Scarlatti wrote a famous piano piece called *The Cat's Fugue,* supposedly representing a cat treading on a keyboard. Ravel's children's opera *L'Enfant et Les Sortilèges* was based on a poem by the delightful writer Colette, another passionate devotee of cats. This opera, which tells how animals, household objects and story-book illustrations take their revenge on a spoiled, thoughtless child, contains a highly amusing duet for male and female cats, and can probably claim to be the most faithful and realistic representation of cat utterance in the realm of music.

There have also been several attempts to portray cats in terms of the dance, and two ballets have

Studies of cats from the sketchbook of Kuniyoshi. (Victoria and Albert Museum)

Illustration from the book 'Portraits of Fourteen Famous Ladies of the Yoshiwara' by Masanobu.

proved especially successful in this respect. Tchaikovsky's *Sleeping Princess* contains a pas-de-deux in the last act for Puss in Boots and the White Cat, and this ballet is firmly established in the repertory of many companies.

More ambitious is *Les Demoiselles de la Nuit*, first performed in Paris in 1948, with music by Jean Françaix. In this ballet, a white cat is transformed into a woman through the love of a human. But the lure of the cat world is too strong, and she returns to the rooftops, while her lover falls to his death pursuing her. The action, the choreography and the music have a wonderful feline intensity.

All in all, the cat can have little reason to complain of the publicity which he is enjoying today. After centuries of neglect, the essayists, poets, journalists, composers, cartoonists and photographers are again 'doing him proud'. All we await now is the first exhibition of paintings by a cat.

Margot Fonteyn and Roland Petit in a pas-de-deux from Les Demoiselles de la Nuit *for which Petit did the choreography.*

The divertissement of Puss in Boots and the White Cat from Tchaikovsky's ballet The Sleeping Beauty.

Cats

A cat can make friends with anything from a beetle to an owl.

and their Animal Companions

Small as a mouse, lofty as a giraffe, the cats take them all in their stride.

Out for a Walk

I had no intention, in writing these pages, to speak ill of dogs. I am, indeed, fully alive to the pleasure of being invited out for a walk by a dog, who, jumping about and running round me with eloquently wagging tail, looks at me with eyes that plainly say 'Are we going to start?' And when we are fairly off, I like this trusty comrade who sets off at railway speed, remembers that his master cannot follow him at this pace, manifests his pleasure by the friendliest movements, and starts off again, barking an inspiriting 'Come on!'

But there is a still greater charm, a more refined pleasure in the company of a cat, whose good pleasure it is to lead his master. The cat does not experience the ambulatory enjoyment peculiar to the dog; or at least it does not appear to do so. It follows the person for whom it has an affection, but always on condition that the walk shall be a short one, and in a quiet place. A thoughtful person who walks in the pleached alleys of an old-fashioned garden, meditatively, book in hand, is particularly agreeable to the refined and delicate animal. Before such a one the cat will run, stop suddenly, and roll himself up on the gravelled path, rubbing his back against it with delight. There he will wait until his master comes up and caresses him, and then start off to go through the same 'high jinks' twenty paces farther on.

(M. Champfleury. *The Cat, Past and Present*)

The Cat's Sagacity

The cat is both curious and sagacious.

Its sagacity I do not think anyone will deny. Here is an instance. Every day, after breakfast, I made it a rule to throw a bit of bread into an adjoining room, as far off as I could, so as to induce my cat to run after it as it rolled away. This custom I kept up for several months, and the cat always regarded that piece of bread as the tit-bit of its dessert. Even after it had eaten meat, it would await with attentive interest the minute when it was to start in pursuit of the morsel of soft bread.

One day I held the coveted scrap in my hand, and swung it about for a long time, while the cat eyed it with a kind of patient eagerness, and then, instead of throwing it into the next room, I threw it behind the upper portion of a picture which was slightly inclined forwards from the wall. The surprise of the cat, who, closely following my movements, had observed the direction in which I threw the bread and its disappearance, was extreme. The uneasy look of the animal indicated its consciousness that a material object traversing space could not be annihilated. For some time the cat considered the matter, then it started off into the next room, evidently guided by the reflection that, the piece of bread having disappeared, it must have gone through the wall.

But the bread had not gone through the wall, and the cat returned, disappointed. The animal's logic was at fault. I again attracted its attention by my gestures, and sent a second piece of bread to join the first behind the picture.

This time the cat jumped upon a divan and went straight to the hiding-place. Having inspected the frame on both sides, it began to manoeuvre so dexterously with its paw that it shifted the lower edge of the picture away from the wall, and thus got at the two pieces of bread.

(M. Champfleury. *The Cat, Past and Present*)

Contentment.

Doubt.

The Moods of Cats

Curiosity.

Tedium.

Mirth.

Reverie.

133

Pussy cat ate the dumplings,
Pussy cat ate the dumplings,
  Mamma stood by,
  And cried, Oh, fie!
Why did you eat the dumplings?

Puss came dancing out of a barn
With a pair of bagpipes under her arm;
She could sing nothing but Fiddle cum fee,
The mouse has married the humble bee.
Pipe, cat—dance, mouse—
We'll have a wedding at our good house.

Cats in Nursery Rhyme

I love little pussy,
Her coat is so warm,
And if I don't hurt her
She'll do me no harm.
So I'll not pull her tail,
Nor drive her away,
But pussy and I
Very gently will play.

Pussy cat, pussy cat,
Where have you been?
I've been to London
To look at the Queen.
Pussy cat, pussy cat,
What did you there?
I frightened a little mouse
Under her chair.

Ding, dong, bell,
Pussy's in the well.
Who put her in?
Little Johnny Green.
Who pulled her out?
Little Tommy Stout.
What a naughty boy was that
To try to drown poor pussy cat,
Who never did him any harm,
And killed the mice in his father's barn.

Dame Trot and her cat
Sat down for a chat;
The Dame sat on this side
And puss sat on that.

Puss, says the Dame,
Can you catch a rat,
Or a mouse in the dark?
Purr, says the cat.

Six little mice sat down to spin;
Pussy passed by and she peeped in.
What are you doing, my little men?
Weaving coats for gentlemen.
Shall I come in and cut off your threads?
No, No, Mistress Pussy, you'd bite off our heads.
Oh, no, I'll not; I'll help you to spin.
That may be so, but you don't come in.

Sing, sing,
What shall I sing?
The cat's run away
With the pudding string!
Do, do,
What shall I do?
The cat's run away
With the pudding too!

Scottish Wild Cat

Siamese kittens

Odd man ou

To a Cat

Stately, kindly, lordly friend
                  Condescend
Here to sit by me, and turn
Glorious eyes that smile and burn,
Golden eyes, love's lustrous meed,
On the golden page I read.

All your wondrous wealth of hair
                  Dark and fair,
Silken-shaggy, soft and bright
As the clouds and beams of night,
Pays my reverent hand's caress
Back with friendlier gentleness.

Dogs may fawn on all and some
                  As they come;
You, a friend of loftier mind,
Answer friends alone in kind.
Just your foot upon my hand
Softly bids it understand.

(Algernon Charles Swinburne)

Burmese

The Burmese is the only natural breed of brown cats. Their glossy coats are deep brown above, merging into a paler brown underneath, and their large and expressive eyes are officially described as Chartreuse Yellow.

During the last few years, an attractive and as yet rare offshoot of the breed has been developed, the so-called Blue Burmese, with a highly-polished silvery coat-colour.

Burmese cats are robust and fearless, active hunters, highly intelligent and lovable household pets. Their flair for self-advertisement even extends to snatching wildly at the sleeves and coats of passers-by.

Keeping a crafty eye on things.

The Personality of Cats

What a piece of work...

The domestic cat is a masterpiece of animal construction, perfect in its combination of efficiency and grace. From the extremities of its sensitive whiskers to the tip of its swishing tail it radiates unruffled assurance and unerring competence. For its relatively small size it is extremely agile and powerful, brain, nerves and muscles coordinated in machine-like precision.

Despite slight physical variations between one breed and another, the cat has most of the characteristics and tendencies possessed by his jungle relatives; the same supple, flexible, low-slung body, the same finely-moulded head, the same long tail which helps to achieve perfect balance. The undersides of his feet are padded and he walks on his toes, sharp claws retracted so as to leave no clear footprints for the benefit of pursuers.

Like lions and tigers, he has thirty adult teeth, and a rough tongue covered with papillae, which enables him to lick bones bare and to remove the last vestige of food from his fur. The fur itself is loose-fitting, tearing away easily in the teeth of an attacker and leaving the flesh untouched.

Like leopards and jaguars, his perceptions and reactions are amazingly swift and acute, whiskers, eyebrows, toes and paws all serving as organs of touch; ears so sensitive as to pick up and accurately locate movements a great distance away; eyes which, whilst not able clearly to distinguish colours, are so

The hunter slinks over the lawn.

139

responsive to light and shade as to endow him with visual powers in the dark far beyond our own; and extra-sensory perceptions which alert him to danger long before any outward sign of it appears.

The cat possesses hundreds of voluntary and involuntary muscles which enable the body to perform the brain's biddings with the minimum of effort and the maximum of efficiency. The cat takes plenty of exercise but never wastes energy unnecessarily. He walks but never runs, and seldom attempts anything which is obviously beyond his grasp or in excess of his powers. He has the ability to relax satisfyingly and completely, and his every action is calculated to promote his own well-being and to fulfil his particular requirements.

The best of both worlds

There is no denying the fact that cats are intensely self-centred creatures, and until we accept that simple truth we cannot begin to live in concord with them. Cat-lovers call them independent, self-reliant, dignified, purposeful and resourceful; those less kindly disposed towards them may find them merely arrogant, disobedient, fickle, unpredictable and ungrateful. They are, of course, all these things and much more. They are simply themselves.

The essential spirit of the cat is admirably captured in Rudyard Kipling's *The Cat that Walked by Himself.* The entire relationship between cats and humans is compressed into these few pages;

Siamese has a dip . . .

. . . Siamese has a lick.

Opening up wide.

A black and white cat at ease on the billiards table.

A Siamese cat stalking its prey in South Africa.

Mother carries Junior back to safety

This cat has learned to pull out the darts for the players.

The milk's arrived, so it's time I came in.

the cat's instinctive refusal to conform, its horror of servility, its nocturnal habits, its cunning, curiosity, sense of expediency, playfulness, love of comfort and insistence on being accepted only on its own terms.

The woman obviously has a soft spot for this independent creature and is content to let it sleep by the fire, lap milk and comfort her baby. But the man's reaction is typical and direct. Instinctively mistrustful, he is seized with a desire to humiliate it, to bend it to his own will, to bring it into line with the already subservient dog, the placid horse and the useful cow. In the end an uneasy compromise is struck but there is no real understanding. We have not really progressed far beyond this stage.

Yet those who genuinely love and care for cats know quite well that if you treat a cat like a cat, and not like a half-witted dog or an unruly child, the relationship will be an adult one, based on mutual respect, and capable of deep loyalty and affection. For cats are not cold, disdainful animals, but keenly appreciate comfort and companionship. Contrary to popular belief, they can easily become fonder of a person than of a place. They know intuitively whether they are really loved and under-

stood, and they have innumerable subtle ways of making known their desires and feelings.

The language of cats is a study in itself. Vocally, it consists of an astonishing jumble of purrs, mews, growls, chirrups, wails, squawks, howls, spits and gurgles. They all signify something—contentment, desire, rage, hunger, discomfort, affection. Though bewildering at first, the meanings soon filter through.

Yet many cats will hardly resort at all to vocal communication either with one another or with humans. They find it far more effective to speak with their eyes, their ears, their tail, their fur or with the entire body. Some of the signs are ambiguous on their own—a twitching tail, for instance, may signify either satisfaction or intense annoyance, but most of them are capable of only one interpretation. A contented cat carries its tail high in the air, but droops it when feeling dissatisfied or off-colour. An angry cat flattens its ears against its head, and pricks them forward when alert and expectant. Rubbing its whiskers against your leg denotes affection, arching the back demonstrates hostility—and every cat adopts its own methods and gestures to make itself better understood.

The late Frank Richards, writer of the famous Greyfriars stories, had an intelligent companion in his cat Sammy.

The cat up the tree watches keenly for anything stirring below.

Well, it was there a moment ago.

Command performances

By one means or another the cat generally manages to get what it wants. Unfortunately it does not pay much heed to the principle of one good turn deserving another. It is futile to expect instant obedience from any cat. Should a cat respond to a command or gesture it is probably because it is suitable, convenient or profitable. It sees no point whatsoever in simple blind obedience.

Many cats will, therefore, perform clever and amusing tricks if they appear to perform a useful function, bring them material benefit or give them enjoyment. Some teach themselves to tap on doors and windows in order to climb in and out, to lift latches, to slide bolts or to press bells. Some learn to extract milk from a bottle or cream from a tin by putting in a paw and licking it clean. Some are naturally imitative and try to answer telephones, to turn taps, to play records, to push trolleys and to sweep floors.

The tape may not be red but a cat sure can get tangled up in it.

Other cats can be taught to beg, roll over, wrestle, box, shake hands or even jump through hoops. Patience, kindness and a titbit at the end can work wonders. But few cats will endure derision or ridicule. They will refuse to perform pointlessly and joylessly and consider it beneath their dignity to be dressed up in fancy costumes. Perhaps they will bear it for the sake of a photographer, but they make it quite clear that they consider it all a pitiful waste of time.

Some cats act perversely for no reason save that known to themselves. They disgrace you in front of your friends, attach themselves to the one person in the room who detests them, and stubbornly refuse to perform those antics in which you coached them so successfully only yesterday.

And most of them refuse point blank to do anything in the least bit clever. They are the ones who patiently wait to be let out but never think of scratching on the door, the ones who will never provide material for a glowing letter to the editor, and who will never hit the headlines in the local paper. In fact, for every cat who can flick a light switch there are five hundred who cannot.

Loves and hates

Every owner is aware that his or her cat is individual and unique. That is the secret of their fascination. So it is impossible to generalise, because all behave differently and have their own special likes and dislikes. One enjoys being scrubbed, another is an expert swimmer, a third will go mad even at the sound of running water. One will chase sparrows, another will play with the canary, a third will treat all birds with equal indifference. There are cats who enjoy listening to classical music, cats who prefer jazz, cats who slink from the room at the first note of any kind of music. This cat enjoys travelling, that one gets sick; this one relishes ice-cream, that one prefers asparagus.

Practically all of them, however, derive deep pleasure from sweet scents and perfumes, and are equally averse to bad smells. Catmint appeals to nearly all, and on fine days they are content to lie about under shrubs and in the midst of sweet-smelling flowers. It is just as well, therefore, to keep them well away from those precious perfume bottles.

All cats, too, are great creatures of habit, inquisitive but not adventurous, and easily upset by any sudden change of routine. Their routes around the house and garden are fixed and unvarying.

Some cats can do tricks, like climbing a ladder —

— or spinning a wicker basket —

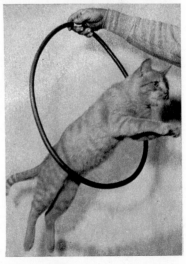

— or jumping through a hoop.

This one is an American cat called Rhubarb, a star of film and television.

145

They have their favourite resting places, whether in front of the fire, in an armchair or perhaps in a cupboard.

For that reason you have to be very careful and considerate when introducing a new pet or moving to a new home. Their memories and homing instincts are fabulous, and there are many amazing stories of cats which have found their way home after journeys of several hundreds of miles, frequently over rough and dangerous terrain.

Not much point in a mouse under glass . . .

Let's see if I can reach them . . .

Now this was a brilliant idea . . .

Come out for a game.

Waking up, in London, on a fine day, your own master – what more could a cat want?

This dockyard cat in London will go to any lengths to get his daily fish.

How bright is a cat?

The comparative intelligence of animals is an absorbing subject for study, and for some it is a lifetime's work. But, true to type, the cat just will not cooperate in this sort of research. The conventional intelligence tests, the intricate mazes, the tuning forks and the coloured discs, are wasted on the cat. For that reason his intelligence is consistently underrated, and much nonsense has been written on the subject.

Every action of the cat points to a high degree of intelligence, if by intelligence we mean using the brain in order to obtain a desired objective. The cat's powers of survival, its ability to fend for itself in times of stress and to minister to its own needs at all times, argue more than purely instinctive reactions.

Such apparently simple actions as leaping on a crowded table or mantelpiece and avoiding all breakable objects, gauging the exact height of a fence or width of a gap—even such negative actions as refusing to attempt more than once a branch which is obviously out of range, or to tackle any creature which has proved its ability to give better than it receives—these seem more certain indications of intelligence than seals balancing balls on their noses, mice finding their way out of mazes, or even dogs counting up to ten.

The trouble is, of course, that we tend to measure animal intelligence by our own. The more humanly an animal behaves, the more intelligent we rate it. This is a false and misleading criterion. Where tricks are concerned, dogs will naturally score over cats every time. But cats are different from dogs, so why should they try to compete on alien territory? And how should you go about testing the intelligence of an 'average' cat? There is no such animal.

St. George Jackson Mivart, the well-known English scientist, who devoted much of his time to the study of cats, wisely observed, 'We cannot, without becoming cats, perfectly understand the cat mind.' That seems to be an admirable conclusion. But that the cat has a mind, and a very individual one at that, let there not be the slightest doubt.

*This Siamese is real
crazy for rhythm.*

These cats sleep and play among the cacti without suffering a scratch.

The Cat Bargains with the Woman

Next day the Cat waited to see if any other Wild Thing would go up to the Cave, but no one moved in the Wet Wild Woods, so the Cat walked there by himself; and he saw the Woman milking the Cow, and he saw the light of the fire in the Cave, and he smelt the smell of the warm white milk.

Cat said, 'O my Enemy and Wife of my Enemy, where did Wild Cow go?'

The Woman laughed and said, 'Wild Thing out of the Wild Woods, go back to the Woods again, for I have braided up my hair, and I have put away the magic blade-bone, and we have no more need of either friends or servants in our Cave.'

Cat said, 'I am not a friend, and I am not a servant. I am the Cat who walks by himself, and I wish to come into your Cave.'

Woman said, 'Then why did you not come with First Friend on the first night?'

Cat grew very angry and said, 'Has Wild Dog told tales of me?'

Then the Woman laughed and said, 'You are the Cat who walks by himself, and all places are alike to you. You are neither a friend nor a servant. You have said it yourself. Go away and walk by yourself in all places alike.'

Then Cat pretended to be sorry and said, 'Must I never come into the Cave? Must I never sit by the warm fire? Must I never drink the warm white milk? You are very wise and very beautiful. You should not be cruel even to a Cat.'

Woman said, 'I knew I was wise, but I did not know I was beautiful. So I will make a bargain with you. If ever I say one word in your praise, you may come into the Cave.'

'And if you say two words in my praise?' said the Cat.

'I never shall,' said the Woman, 'but if I say two words in your praise, you may sit by the fire in the Cave.'

'And if you say three words?' said the Cat.

'I never shall,' said the Woman, 'but if I say three words in your praise, you may drink the warm white milk three times a day for always and always and always.'

Then the Cat arched his back and said, 'Now let the Curtain at the mouth of the Cave, and the Fire at the back of the Cave, and the Milk-pots that stand beside the Fire, remember what my Enemy and the Wife of my Enemy has said.' And he went away through the Wet Wild Woods waving his wild tail and walking by his wild lone.

(Rudyard Kipling. *The Cat that Walked by Himself*)

Why bother to prove a cat's intelligence?

Just look at his expression.

Answers to the True or False Quiz

1. True 2. True 3. True 4. False 5. False

6. True 7. True 8. True 9. False 10. True

11. True 12. False 13. False 14. False 15. False

16. True 17. False 18. True 19. True 20. False

Acknowledgements

Acknowledgements are gratefully due to the following for permission to reproduce original photographs. The numbers refer to pages:

A.F.A. 103(C); H. Armstrong-Roberts 13, 25(L), 30(T), 31(T), 87(BL), 88(T), 101(B), 102, 106(T), 133(BL), 144(B); Barnabys Picture Library 10(T), 14(TR), 14(B), 29(B), 31(BR), 42, 61, 64(R), 69(R), 70(B), 79, 81(B), 90(T), 115, 138(TL), 138(BL); Barratts Photo Press 52(T), 53(T), 69(L); Black Star 1, 15(BL), 16(TR), 17, 19, 26(T), 32(B), 65(BL), 67, 68(R), 72(T), 77(B), 78(BR), 87(T), 87(CL), 87(C), 94(BR), 97(CR), 104, 120, 133(TR), 140(BL), 144(T), 150(R); Florence Bone 26(B), 96, 106(C), 119(TR), 119(C), 119(BR); British Museum 6, 7, 12, 43, 44(B), 46(C), 46(B), 123; Jane Burton 103(TR); Camera Clix 20, 21, 41, 59, 60, 62, 80, 81(T), 82, 117, 118, 136(B); Camera Press 10(B), 14(TC), 16(CL), 25(BR), 46(T), 65(T), 68(L), 71(B), 76(T), 77(T), 95, 98, 110(B), 111(T), 112(T), 113(L), 114, 116, 119(TL), 130(BR), 131(TL), 131(B), 133(TL), 139(B), 148(T), 149(B); Central Press Photos 33(B), 55(R), 99, 138(TR); Lynwood M. Chace 87(CR); Courtauld Institute of Art 126(C), 126(B); Daily Sketch 110(T); Vera Elkan 133(CR), 140(BR); Reginald Eyre, Camera Press 89(TL), 91(T); Reginald Eyre, Photo Centre 15(BR), 89(BL); Fox Photos 36(TR), 105(R), 131(CR), 149(T); Paul Hamlyn Library 8, 45(B), 47, 148(B); E.O. Hoppé 84, 93(C), 106(B), 130(BL), 140(TR); Keystone Press Agency 9, 16(TL), 22, 23(T), 36(B), 39, 40, 49(CR), 51, 52(C), 53(C), 53(B), 55(TL), 56(T), 57(T), 64(L), 74, 108(L), 112(BR), 119(BL), 130(T), 131(CL), 143(T); Kevin MacDonnell 14(TL), 37(C), 44(T), 45(T), 75(B), 91(R), 133(CL); National Gallery, London 122, 124, 126(T); L. Hugh Newman 140 (TL); Photo Centre 129(T); Photo Researchers 135; Pictorial Press 92, 97(CL), 150(L); Paul Popper 15(CL), 16(CR), 31(BL), 34(TC), 34(B), 37(BL), 37(BR), 49(CL), 50, 55(BL), 57(B), 70(TL), 70(TR), 71(T), 72(BL), 72(BR), 73, 76(TL), 76(TR), 76(B), 78(BL), 88(B), 89(R), 91(CL), 93(T), 93(B), 94(L), 94(TR), 100, 101(TL), 101(TR), 103(TL), 103(B), 105(L), 130(C), 131(TR), 136(T), 139(TL), 139(TR), 141, 145, 146, 147; Radio Times Hulton Picture Library 37(TR), 49(BL), 49(BR), 127; Houston Rogers 129(B); R.S.P.C.A. 111(BR); Sport and General Press Agency 16(B), 24, 29(T), 32(T), 34(BC), 49(BC), 52(B), 54, 56(B), 58, 75(T), 78(T), 90(B), 137; Stoke Newington Observer 111(BL); W. Suschitzky 11, 14(C), 15(T), 25(TR), 27(T), 35, 36(TL), 49(T), 66, 91(BL), 97(T), 97(BL), 97(BR), 143(B), 151; Syndication International 2, 15(CR), 27(B), 28, 30(B), 34(T), 37(TL), 75(C), 85, 87(BR), 90(C), 108(R), 112(BL), 113(R), 133(BR), 142; The Times 138(BR); United Press International (U.K.) 65(BR); Victoria and Albert Museum 125, 128; V. Watson 138(C); Welwyn Times 109.

Acknowledgements are also made to the following for permission to reproduce copyright material:

Messrs. George Allen & Unwin Ltd., for an extract from Karel Čapek's *I Had a Dog and a Cat;* Messrs. Faber and Faber Ltd. for the poem 'The Naming of Cats' from *Old Possum's Book of Practical Cats;* Messrs. William Heinemann Ltd. for the poem 'To a Cat' from *Swinburne's Collected Poetical Works;* Messrs. A. A. Knopf, New York, for an extract from Carl van Vechten's *Tiger in the House;* Mrs. G. Bambridge, Messrs. Macmillan & Co. Ltd. and the Macmillan Co. of Canada for an extract taken from Rudyard Kipling's *Just So Stories;* Mrs. W. B. Yeats and Messrs. Macmillan & Co. Ltd. for the poem 'The Cat and the Moon' from *Collected Poems of W. B. Yeats.*